Not by Bread Alone

*One does not live by bread alone, but by every word
that comes from the mouth of God.*

—Matthew 4:4

Not by Bread Alone

Recipes and Reflections
for Christian Cooks

MARY ANN MCGIVERN

ACTA Publications
Chicago, Illinois

Not by Bread Alone:
Recipes and Reflections for Christian Cooks

By Mary Ann McGivern

Cover Design by Tom A. Wright

Page Design by Patrice J. Tuohy

Typesetting by Garrison Publications

Published by   ACTA Publications
Assisting Christians to Act
4848 North Clark Street
Chicago, IL 60640
800-397-2282

Library of Congress Catolog Number: 98-70832
ISBN: 0-87946-181-0
Printed in Canada
02 01 00 99 98   5 4 3 2 1

Contents

INTRODUCTION *11*

Winter: Ordinary Time

PREPARE THE WAY OF THE LORD *13*

SAVOR THE NEW YEAR   *Blue Cheese, Mushroom and
Caramelized Onion Pizza* *14*

GRANT US GOOD GIFTS   *Basic Creole Fish Stew* *16*

DARE TO BE DIFFERENT   *Pasta with Shrimp and Avocado* . . . *18*

FEEDING OTHERS   *Black Bean Soup* *20*

TRICKSTERS CONSIDERED   *Eggplant Swiss* *22*

UPSET THE NATURAL ORDER   *Spinach Burritos* *24*

STURDY PEOPLE, STURDY FOOD   *Potato Pancakes* *26*

BUSY LIVES, JOYFUL HEARTS   *Spaghetti Casserole* *28*

HONOR THOSE WHO PROVIDE FOR US   *Vegetarian Chili* . . . *30*

Lent and Easter

BE LEAVEN FOR THE KINGDOM *33*

EAT OF THE LIVING BREAD   *How to Make a Starter* *34*

THE SECRET OF FASTING   *Plain White Bread* *36*

ALL IN A DAY'S WORK   *Cloverleaf Rolls* *38*

THE BAKER'S DISCIPLINE   *Using a Bread Machine* *40*

BREAD BUILDS STRONG BODIES   *Multigrain Bread* *42*

GIVE THANKS   *Pizza Crust* *44*

DISTRIBUTE THE PLENTY   *Irish Soda Bread—Russian Soda Bread—
Italian Soda Bread—Norwegian Julekaka* *46*

TASTE AND SEE   *Corn Tortillas* *48*

POWER PLAYS   *Muffins with Oatmeal, Walnuts and Dates* . . . *50*

ONE BREAD, ONE BODY   *Honey Bran Muffins with Cheddar Cheese* . . . *52*

COMMUNITY BUILDING   *Fast Buttermilk Yeast Rolls* *54*

PASSOVER, HOLY THURSDAY: CHOSEN FOR LOVE   *Leg of Lamb* . . . *56*

Good Friday: We Know Not What We Do   *Hot Cross Buns* 58
Holy Saturday: Quiet Preparation   *Hard-Boiled Eggs* 60
Easter: Recognizing God among Us   *Challah Bread* 62

Spring: Ordinary Time

The Eye of the Beholder 65
The Good Earth   *Chili Rellenos* 66
Rain with Justice   *Pasta Primavera* 68
Cast a Wide Net   *Fried Catfish* 70
Be Like Little Children   *Baked Salmon with Tomato-Basil Sauce* 72
A Coin of the Realm   *Imitation Crab Spinach Salad* 74
Infants in Christ   *Raspberry Borscht* 76
Bounty   *Italian Bean Salad* 78
Witness God's Creation   *Bean Sprouts—Egg Foo Yung* 80

Summer: Ordinary Time

Come to the Banquet 83
Bite into Life   *Roasted Garlic and Brie* 84
Sweet Hot Times   *Mango Salsa and Chips* 86
Wisdom Wins the Day   *Melitzanosalata (Eggplant Salad)* 88
A Dose of Vinegar   *Tuna Aspic* 90
More Vinegar   *Sautéed Spinach with Balsamic Syrup* 92
Mind Your Manners   *Watermelon with Olives and Feta Cheese* 94
All I Have Is Yours   *Scallops with Lettuce Salad* 96
Clean Hearts   *Fresh Tomatoes and Roasted Garlic Pasta* 98
Wine to Gladden the Heart   *Shrimp with Wild Rice* 100
Drink to Love   *Berries and Creamy Yogurt Cheese* 102

Autumn: Ordinary Time

Fruitful Endeavors 105
Labor Pains   *Granola* 106
Honor the Saints   *Pureed, Preserved Ginger—Ginger Carrots* 108

EXPERIENCE OF EVIL *Stuffed Squash with Orange-Ginger Sauce* *110*
THE FOOLISH FARMER *Stuffed Eggplant with Roasted Pepper Sauce* *112*
OURS FOR THE TAKING *Tomato Seasoning Mix—*
    Quick Pasta Sauce *114*
FAMINE TACTICS *Vegetarian Lasagna* *116*
EXCESS *Baked Ziti* *118*
LOVE THE STRANGER *Chitterlings and Hog Maws—Turkey Gumbo—*
    Cranberry Soup *120*

Advent

KNOWING OURSELVES, KNOWING GOD *123*
GOD THE COOK *Quiche with Crab* *124*
WHO IS GOD? *Roast Pork in Milk* *126*
RECOGNIZING POWER *Sweet Potatoes with Cider Vinaigrette* *128*
PAY ATTENTION *Argentinian Stew* *130*
ESSENTIAL TRUTHS *Pasta with Anchovies* *132*
THE SPICES OF OUR LIVES *Rice with Stir-Fried Chicken* *134*
TAKE A GOOD LOOK *Stuffed Grape Leaves* *136*

Christmas

GOOD THINGS AND GLAD TIDINGS *139*
SCENTED MEMORIES *Very Low Fat Pumpkin Pie* *140*
HOW TO MAKE "MERRY" *Traditional Fruitcake* *142*
FEED MY SHEEP *Healthy Applesauce Cake* *144*
EATING WITH SINNERS *Chocolate Chip Cookies* *146*
THE LORD IS SWEET *Chocolate Chocolate Sweets* *148*
BE READY FOR ACTION *Lemon Poppy Seed Pound Cake* *150*
THE COOK'S SIMPLE PRAYER *Fruit Crumble* *152*

ACKNOWLEDGMENTS *155*
INDEX TO RECIPES *157*
INDEX TO SCRIPTURE PASSAGES *159*

For Julia Costello McGivern,
who taught me to bake bread

Introduction

WHO AMONG US are the blessed who toss together delicious meals with lightning speed day after day, never losing our enthusiasm or creative touch? We want to do the best for our families, but often we run out of ideas, get tired of eating our own cooking and have bad cooking habits. Alas, meal planning is an onerous task for most cooks. We struggle against boredom, lack of time and ingredients, and the high cost of food.

Not by Bread Alone: Recipes and Reflections for Christian Cooks won't solve these problems with a few magic recipes and meditations, but it may help cooks think differently about the task by reminding us that meals are a gift to ourselves and those we love and that preparing nourishment for the body can be a time for feeding the soul.

This is neither a gourmet cookbook nor a scholarly analysis of scripture. The recipes and meditations are simple and seasonal. The meals have been tested on children as well as adults. Most of the recipes are a little off the beaten track, calling for ingredients like eggplant, black beans, basil, ginger and lots of garlic. They are mainly vegetarian and low in fat and, unless otherwise noted, egg substitutes and nonfat dairy products may be used. Some ingredients are optional; you're encouraged to use your culinary imagination. The reflections are meant to help us get meals on the table with a minimum of anxiety and a maximum of inner satisfaction.

Even in Jesus' time, getting the food on the table must have been a major source of worry, because Jesus tells us to "consider the ravens: they neither sow nor reap" (Luke 12:24). In the Gospels of Matthew, Mark and Luke, the point Jesus makes to the apostles after feeding the multitudes (twice in Matthew and Mark) is that they shouldn't worry about where their dinner is coming from—God will provide. (All well and good for the apostles, who had Jesus around to multiply loaves and fishes for them!)

But Jesus means what he says. Over and over the gospels use the image of food to instruct us to rely on God—telling us to pray for our daily bread, that we don't live by bread alone, that the kingdom of God is like yeast. Matthew, Mark, Luke and John describe an abundance of food—not just seven different accounts of the loaf and fish multiplication, but one account of making wine from water at Cana, two of filling the fishers' nets to the breaking point, and the Magnificat's assurance that God has filled the hungry with good things.

How do we reconcile our daily toil in the kitchen with Jesus' injunction not to be anxious? By chewing on Jesus' words, letting them marinate in the refrigerator and simmer on the back burner, mulling them like spiced wine. That Jesus should tell us not to worry about where our next meal is coming from is as great an upheaval of the natural order as when he dined with tax collectors and sinners or found the coin to pay Caesar in the mouth of a fish. When we look directly at Jesus' teaching, it turns the rest of our world upside down.

Scripture is the yeast that forms our faith and shapes our lives. These meditations link scripture to our recipes, meal planning and food preparation. The result, I hope, will be mindful meal preparation—cooking that becomes in itself a lifting of the mind and heart to God.

Winter: Ordinary Time

PREPARE THE WAY OF THE LORD

When the disciples reached the other side, they had forgotten to bring any bread. Jesus said to them, "Watch out and beware of the yeast of the Pharisees and Sadducees." They said to one another, "It is because we have brought no bread." And becoming aware of it, Jesus said, "You of little faith, why are you talking about having no bread? Do you still not perceive? Do you not remember the five loaves for the five thousand, and how many baskets you gathered? Or the seven loaves for the four thousand, and how many baskets you gathered? How could you fail to perceive that I was not speaking about bread? Beware of the yeast of the Pharisees and Sadducees!" Then they understood that he had not told them to beware of the yeast of bread, but of the teachings of the Pharisees and Sadducees.—Matt. 16:5-12

The poor apostles. Yes, they had seen Jesus feed 9,000 people, but they were hungry at that moment, and they knew that they were with a man who had fasted for 40 days and then resisted the temptation to turn the stones into bread. They may also have known, as many scholars suspect, that the miracles of the loaves and fishes were really the miracles of people pulling hidden food from their pockets and sharing it. The apostles had cause to fear they were going to go hungry. Sure enough, Jesus used the occasion to talk about false teachings. He let them gnaw on philosophical truths. The hungry apostles should have remembered to pack the bread.

It is the old Christian paradox of good works and faith, expressed here as the daily necessity to prepare food like wise serpents over against reliance, like trusting doves, on the providence of God. Even as we plan and prepare meals, we pray to the Father for our daily bread. It is a mystery that surrounds our kitchen tasks, holding us in faith. It is also a divine joke on anxious cooks who lose confidence in God because we know the food won't get on the table without us. Perhaps, as in the miracles of the loaves and fishes, it is a matter of God having confidence in us.

SAVOR THE NEW YEAR

"For everyone will be salted with fire. Salt is good, but if salt has lost its saltiness, how can you season it? Have salt in yourselves, and be at peace with one another."—Mark 9:49-50

Salt is a flavor enhancer and preservative. Here Jesus enjoins us to be the salt, improving the quality of life and so gaining peace. This is a call to savor life. We may be reducing the salt in our diet, but we still want to enhance the flavor of our meals and our days.

When we pause during the coming year to honor our children's triumphs, we will increase their pleasure. Our sorrow at cruelties done to even a faraway neighbor will enhance the prayer of believers that sustains those who suffer. Long and careful thought will season our political decisions. Giving money to charities will preserve their good works. Creating beauty anywhere—a delicious meal, a song, a flower garden—will improve the flavors of life and preserve its goodness.

Jesus is the fire that has salted us. He renews our savor when we salt the world with his love and goodness. New Year's Eve is a great time to renew our resolve to be more loving.

The 11-year-old son of a friend of mine read in a school magazine that children don't like strong seasonings because they have many more taste buds than adults and are more sensitive to spices. Children might not like this zesty pizza. It's a better choice for adult guests on New Year's Eve than at the supper table. It's an adult pizza, for adult tastes, just as this scripture passage is for adults.

Blue Cheese, Mushroom and Caramelized Onion Pizza

2½ tbs. olive oil
2 large onions, thinly sliced
(about 5 cups)
2 tbs. brown sugar
8 oz. shitake or portobello
mushrooms, stemmed,
caps sliced
1 12-inch baked pizza crust
(to bake your own, see
p. 45)
8 oz. blue cheese, crumbled
1 tbs. fresh thyme, chopped
or 1 tsp. dried thyme

Heat 1 tbs. olive oil in a large skillet over medium heat. Sauté the onions until they're translucent, about 10 minutes. Add sugar, reduce the heat to medium-low and sauté for another 20 minutes. In another skillet, heat the remaining oil in a skillet over high heat. Add mushrooms and sauté until limp, approximately 8 minutes. Season with salt and pepper.

Place the pizza crust on a baking sheet. Sprinkle the blue cheese and thyme over the crust. Layer the onions onto the cheese. Top with mushrooms. Bake the pizza at 450° until the cheese bubbles, about 15 minutes. Cool in pan 5 minutes. Cut and serve. *Serves 4.*

It has to be love, love that overcomes fear, that shares and makes sure that nobody is hungry, that unites us when we learn about each other, when we share our gifts, when we believe in each other, when we take time to listen to each other, and to share our stories, our arts, our customs, our traditions, when we break bread together.

THEA BOWMAN, from *Shooting Star*

GRANT US GOOD GIFTS

"Is there anyone among you, if your child asks for a fish, will give a snake instead of a fish? Or if the child asks for an egg, will give a scorpion? If you then, who are evil, know how to give good gifts to your children, how much more will the heavenly Father give the Holy Spirit to those who ask him!"
—Luke 11:11-13

Pray unceasingly. Ask for what you need, ask for what you want. Pray for wisdom, understanding and fortitude. Pray for others—loved ones, acquaintances, strangers. Pray for world peace, an end to hunger and a more just world. Pray always. Why? Because your prayers will be answered. Jesus is very clear on this point. Prayer works.

And just as God will grant good gifts to us, so must we give good gifts to others. One gift cooks can give to those for whom they prepare meals is healthy, balanced ingredients. Avoid using hefty amounts of salt, oil, mayonnaise, cream, sour cream, meat, canned soups and vegetables with high sodium and fat content.

In moderation, these things don't do much harm. But we could stand to learn new habits and give ourselves and our families a taste for beans, yogurt and pasta in place of baked potatoes with sour cream and cauliflower in cheese sauce.

Be experimental, imaginative and steadfast in your cooking as well as in your spiritual life.

BASIC CREOLE FISH STEW

1 medium onion, sliced
2 cloves garlic, minced
2 tbs. olive oil
1 can tomatoes (29 oz.)
1 tsp. oregano
½ tsp. curry
½ tsp. salt
pepper
1 lb. fish fillets (orange
    roughy, butterfish,
    catfish, etc.), cut into
    small pieces

Brown the onion and garlic in olive oil in a large skillet. Add the tomatoes and seasonings; bring the mixture to a boil. Add the fish and simmer gently about 20 minutes until the fish is cooked through. Serve over cooked noodles or rice. *Serves 4.*

I know of no other outdoor sport which can furnish me with so much pleasure as foraging wild food which can be made into exquisite dishes to share with family and friends.

EUELL GIBBONS, from *Stalking the Wild Asparagus*

DARE TO BE DIFFERENT

Now John wore clothing of camel's hair with a leather belt around his waist, and his food was locusts and wild honey.—Matt. 3:4

In midwinter, thoughts about John the Baptist's life in the desert have a certain attraction. The white sand and hot sun could scrub a soul clean. The wild honey sounds delicious, though collecting it might be risky. Locusts are a drawback; perhaps they are an acquired taste or perhaps they taste a little like chicken or shrimp.

Locusts and wild honey were exotic to the Jews and Greeks. After all, most of them lived in cities, not the desert. If wild honey was available in the marketplace, it would have been expensive. And Matthew, Mark and Luke—who all describe John's cuisine—probably never ate a locust in their lives.

The point was not that John suffered at meals, but that he was different—as different in what he ate as he was in his dress, his critique of society and his willingness to give way before Jesus.

We are each unique and our differences are to be treasured. A diverse society is a strong society. John's great gift was that by knowing who he was, he was able to recognize the Savior—a very different kind of man. John was lean and sharp-tongued, while Jesus was gentler and more powerful. Maybe we're plumper and more soft-spoken—it doesn't matter. What's important is that we love the friends we know and the strangers we don't know. It's important that we celebrate diversity, enjoying our differences and recognizing Jesus' presence in the farthest neighbor.

The pasta recipe below is a festive dish designed to get us through the dreary cold grey of February. Kids like it, so it's a good choice for a birthday or Sunday dinner. Unlike our image of John the Baptist's meals, there's nothing Spartan about this recipe. Its culinary purpose is aesthetic, not ascetic.

So splurge. Buy some shrimp and avocado and startle the relatives coming for the birthday dinner. And give thanks for John the Baptist, the hero of exotic menus.

Pasta with Shrimp and Avocado

9 oz. fettucini
1 tbs. butter
1 tsp. fresh garlic, minced
1 tbs. fresh parsley, minced
1 lb. shrimp, peeled and deveined
2 tbs. dry vermouth or white wine
3 tbs. butter
½ cup heavy cream or half-and-half (the fat content is needed to thicken the sauce)
¼ cup parmesan cheese, grated
pinch of crushed red pepper flakes
¼ tsp. salt
⅛ tsp. ground black pepper
1 avocado, peeled, pitted and sliced

Add fettucini to boiling water. Cook *al dente* (until tender but slightly chewy). Drain.

Cook the garlic in butter for 1 minute in a large skillet. Add the parsley, shrimp and vermouth and cook for 2 minutes, stirring constantly. Do not overcook. Transfer all of this to a small bowl.

In the same skillet heat the rest of the butter, reduce the heat to low and add the cream, parmesan and red pepper flakes. Cook until the cheese melts and the sauce is smooth (about 5 minutes), stirring constantly. Stir in the salt and pepper.

Place the fettucini on a serving dish; add the shrimp mixture, avocado and sauce; toss gently. *Serves 4.*

The discovery of a new dish does more for human happiness than the discovery of a new star.

Anthelme Brillat-Savarin

FEEDING OTHERS

When he came to the house [of Jairus], he did not allow anyone to enter with him except Peter, John and James, and the child's father and mother. They were all weeping and wailing for her; but he said, "Do not weep; for she is not dead but sleeping." And they laughed at him, knowing that she was dead. But he took her by the hand and called out, "Child, get up!" Her spirit returned and she got up at once. Then he directed them to give her something to eat.
—Luke 8:51-55

The ending to this miracle, the raising back to life of Jairus' daughter, is decidedly anticlimactic. "Give her something to eat," Jesus instructs. The girl was probably given a cup of soup, hugged, cried over, told how sick she'd been and urged to rest, to eat more, to thank Jesus, to give kisses all around. What did she make of the miracle? Did it change her life? Did she gain compassion for the hungry and those near death? Could she be counted on forever after to nurse the sick and feed the beggars who came to her door? I hope so.

Offering food is the most ordinary expression of our concern for one another. Jesus uses our worries about where the next meal will come from to teach us confidence in God, but when a child is raised from the dead, even Jesus counts on the cook to conclude the miracle.

The act of feeding others changes our lives incrementally. Every day brings opportunities to exercise generosity and gratitude. But we miss the obvious, the same way Jairus and his household missed it. Let's try to pay a little better attention to our loved ones at our dinner table and to the strangers on the street corner.

Black Bean Soup

16 oz. black turtle beans
(or 2 cans of black beans)
6-8 cups vegetable
(or chicken) broth
2 tbs. butter or olive oil
1 cup onion, chopped
1 cup celery, chopped
1 cup carrots, chopped
1 cup potatoes, shredded
1 bay leaf
2 cloves garlic, minced
1 tsp. oregano
½ tsp. freshly ground pepper
3 tbs. fresh lemon juice
(fresh lemon is the key to a great, not merely good, black bean soup)
lemon slices
yogurt or sour cream

Rinse the beans. In a large stock pot, cover the beans with water and soak overnight. Drain the beans and return them to the stock pot. Add the broth and heat to boiling. Reduce the heat and simmer, covered, for 3 to 4 hours.

If you use canned beans, drain the canned beans, add the broth and heat to boiling. Reduce heat and simmer for 5 minutes.

In a large skillet, melt the butter and sauté the onions, celery and carrots for 3 to 5 minutes or until crisp-tender. Add to the beans along with the potatoes, bay leaf, garlic, oregano and pepper. Stir well and simmer, covered, for 45 minutes or until the vegetables are tender. Stir lemon juice into the soup just before serving. Pour the soup into individual bowls and garnish with lemon slices and yogurt or sour cream.

Give me neither poverty nor riches; feed me with the food that I need.
PROVERBS 30:8

TRICKSTERS CONSIDERED

"Consider the ravens: they neither sow nor reap, they have neither storehouse nor barn and yet God feeds them. Of how much more value are you than the birds!"—Luke 12:24

Consider the ravens, bigger than crows, living among mountains and skyscrapers. They are tricksters who work in pairs, double-teaming an eagle out of the fish he just caught and defying scarecrows in an open field. They work hard for their food, even if they don't sow the seeds. Surely Jesus had watched them, knowing they weren't helpless chicks but resourceful opportunists.

We live, most of us, at a great distance from nature. Perhaps we hear the caw of ravens or crows; but few of us have ever seen these rascals stealing corn from a mill. Ravens live for us in fairy tales, poetry and here in scripture where, despite all their clever work, it is God who feeds them. This is the mystery, the point Jesus never tires of making. It is God who saves. Even the brazen ravens are a sign of God's love for us.

The recipe that follows, Eggplant Swiss, reminds me of the trickster ravens, because eggplants have no relation to eggs—unless you dream of giant purple hens. Yet eggplant is so hearty that it can trick you into thinking you're eating meat.

EGGPLANT SWISS

1 eggplant, medium to large
3 cloves garlic
3 tbs. olive oil
½ lb. Swiss cheese, sliced
2 cups pasta sauce
(see recipe on p. 115,
or use canned tomato
sauce)
12 oz. pasta (penne is often
used)
parmesan cheese

Add pasta to boiling water. Cook *al dente* (until tender but slightly chewy). Drain.

Wash the eggplant, remove the stem, make a shallow, lengthwise slit in the skin and microwave for 5 minutes.

Mince the garlic and sauté it for 1 minute in a large skillet. Slice the microwaved eggplant into long thin strips and add it to the oil and garlic. (If you don't have a microwave, slice raw eggplant into strips, ½ inch by ½ inch, and sauté it with the garlic for 10 to 15 minutes in a skillet.) Add tomato sauce, cover and simmer on the top of the stove for 20 to 30 minutes.

Five minutes before serving, layer the Swiss cheese over the simmering eggplant. Serve over the pasta with parmesan cheese. *Serves 4.*

A note on eggplant: *If it has been on the market shelf too long, it may taste bitter. Some cooks slice it raw, soak it in salted water for 20 minutes, and then rinse it to remove the bitterness. Perhaps I've just been lucky, but my microwave strategy hasn't given me a bitter eggplant yet.*

UPSET THE NATURAL ORDER

The day was drawing to a close, and the twelve came to him and said, "Send the crowd away, so that they may go into the surrounding villages and countryside, to lodge and get provisions; for we are here in a deserted place." But he said to them, "You give them something to eat." They said, "We have no more than five loaves and two fish—unless we are to go and buy food for all these people." For there were about five thousand men. And he said to his disciples, "Make them sit down in groups of about fifty each." They did so and made them all sit down. And taking the five loaves and the two fish, he looked up to heaven, and blessed and broke them, and gave them to the disciples to set before the crowd. And all ate and were filled. What was left over was gathered up, twelve baskets of broken pieces.—Luke 9:12-17

It would appear that Jesus was teasing the apostles—and that they, with their offer to purchase groceries, were in turn teasing him. It must have been an exciting moment. The apostles were confident that they were going to see Jesus exercise his power to upset the natural order by feeding the hungry.

All his life, Jesus upset the natural order. He turned life upside down. Here the apostles were worried that 5,000 men (plus women and children) would have no supper or beds for the night.

It was a heaven-sent opportunity for Jesus to teach them and us that God cares for us and that our blessings come from God. I said in the introduction that many scholars think the miracle was in inducing all Jesus' followers to share the food they'd brought with them. Similarly, it is through our hands that Jesus continues to feed the hungry.

These spinach burritos are a quick meal that will feed and fill an entire basketball team. But they don't appear miraculously. The groceries must be purchased and the food cooked. That's the natural order of things. What's supernatural is when we share the food of our table with those who are hungry.

Spinach Burritos

2 cloves garlic, minced
1 tsp. olive oil
1 small onion, diced
1 lb. fresh spinach or
    1 12-oz. pkg. frozen
10 large flour tortillas
2 cans nonfat refried beans
1 lb. mild cheddar cheese,
    shredded (less if
    beef or fish is used)
½ lb. ground beef, browned
    (optional)
½ lb. fish, cooked (optional)
salsa (see mango salsa recipe
    on p. 87 or 1 jar
    prepared)
1 avocado, sliced
sour cream or plain yogurt

Sauté the cloves of minced garlic in olive oil for 1 minute. Add chopped onion and spinach. Cover and simmer over low heat until the spinach is limp and the onion is translucent.

Spread the refried beans on the tortillas. Add the spinach mixture and cheese, or, if you want heartier burritos, add browned ground beef or cooked fish and a little less cheese. Roll. Place side by side in an 8-by-12-inch baking pan. Cover lightly with salsa. Bake for 15 minutes at 400°. (Or place on individual plates and microwave for 2 minutes each.) Serve with salsa, avocado and a dollop of sour cream or yogurt.

If you use fish, it should be boneless and precooked in the microwave oven for 2 minutes or simmered in the skillet with the spinach. *Serves 5 hungry kids or 8 adults.*

We should ask forgiveness from the poor for the bread we give them.
Saint Vincent de Paul

STURDY PEOPLE, STURDY FOOD

Now Simon's mother-in-law was in bed with a fever, and they told him about her at once. He came and took her by the hand and lifted her up. Then the fever left her, and she began to serve them.—Mark 1:30-31

When Simon Peter's mother-in-law was healed, she got up and made dinner. She's one of the sturdy women who fed Jesus and his disciples, mended their clothes, sheltered them, visited them in prison, nursed them in illness and buried them. Her response to Jesus' healing touch was to go back to work, to return to her daily tasks. This is a sign of Jesus' complete healing power—no lingering pain, no gradual resumption of duties. She was fully recovered and up to the tasks at hand. Jesus made her whole. For Christians, Jesus is our strength. Christians are sturdy people who get the job done.

That's the sort of woman I'd like to think Peter's mother-in-law was: one who gets the job done. Work needs to be done, and we participate in the providence of God by doing it instead of waiting for miracles. Potato pancakes also get the job done. They provide a hearty meal for sturdy people.

POTATO PANCAKES

**6 medium potatoes, grated
 (peeled or unpeeled)**
1 onion, grated
1 carrot, grated
¼ cup milk or buttermilk
2 eggs, beaten
1 cup flour (white or wheat)
salt and pepper
oil for frying
sour cream or low fat yogurt
applesauce

Drain the grated vegetables in a colander. Then mix them with the milk and eggs in a large bowl. Add flour and stir thoroughly. Add salt and pepper to taste.

Coat a skillet with a thin cover of oil. Heat it and spoon in about 3 tablespoons of mix per pancake. Turn them when their bottoms are golden brown. Serve with sour cream or low fat yogurt and applesauce. *Serves 6.*

Lord God, you are indeed the loving Father who provides us with food for body and spirit. Make our work fruitful and give us a rich harvest. Help us bring you glory by using well the good things we receive from you. We ask this through Christ our Lord. Amen

PRAYER OVER THE GIFTS, from the *Mass for Productive Land*

BUSY LIVES, JOYFUL HEARTS

*All who believed were together and had all things in common; they would sell
their possessions and goods and distribute the proceeds to all, as any had need.
Day by day, as they spent much time together in the temple, they broke bread
at home and ate their food with glad and generous hearts, praising God and
having the goodwill of all the people.*—Acts 2:44-47

We are busy people and often complain about how much we have to
do. It turns out that the early Christians were busy, too, selling their
property, distributing the proceeds and forming communities, while
still earning a living, shopping at the market and cooking meals at home.
They had the same 24 hours we have—without central heating, gas stoves or
washing machines. Their lives were at least as full as ours. But they were
joyful.

God invented casseroles for people who are out of the house all day,
whether at work, chauffeuring children or in church. This spaghetti casserole
can also be carried to meetings and gatherings for a potluck supper. So take a
deep breath, focus on the task at hand and find joy in the community who
will sit down and eat this meal.

SPAGHETTI CASSEROLE

1 lb. spaghetti, broken into two-inch pieces
2 tbs. margarine
⅔ cup cheese, grated (American, Monterey Jack, or mild cheddar)
½ tsp. pepper
2 eggs, well beaten
2 tbs. olive oil
1 medium onion, chopped
1 clove garlic, minced
1 lb. mushrooms, sliced
½ cup green pepper, chopped
2 cups pasta sauce (see recipe on p. 115 or use prepared tomato sauce)
½ tsp. oregano
1 lb. cottage cheese
8 oz. mozzarella cheese, shredded

Boil the spaghetti according to package directions. Drain and cool it slightly. In a large bowl, mix the spaghetti with the margarine, grated cheese, pepper and eggs.

Sauté the onion and garlic in olive oil until the onion is translucent. Add the mushrooms and green peppers and sauté for 1 more minute. Drain. Stir in the pasta sauce and oregano.

Grease a 12-by-9-inch pan with nonstick spray. Layer the spaghetti and cheese mixture, the cottage cheese and the pasta sauce mixture. Bake at 350° for 30 minutes. Spread mozzarella cheese over top and bake an additional 10 minutes. Let stand 15 minutes before cutting. *Serves 8.*

A home is no home unless it contains food and fire for the mind as well as for the body.

MARGARET FULLER

HONOR THOSE WHO PROVIDE FOR US

"Let Pharaoh proceed to appoint overseers over the land, and take one fifth of the produce of the land of Egypt during the seven plenteous years."
—Gen. 41:34

We take fresh vegetables for granted, even in midwinter. It's unimaginable that beans or canned tomatoes would ever be missing from super-market shelves. We seldom think of the Greek farmers pressing their olives for oil, the Mexican celery cutters, the cannery workers, or the truckers who deliver this wealth of foodstuffs to our grocers.

Hundreds of thousands of agricultural laborers, food-service workers and delivery men and women around the world stand between us and famine—ensuring food for the cities despite flood, drought, frost or fire. A vast food-processing network undergirds our civilization, and we are its beneficiaries.

In Egypt, the Pharaoh was advised by Joseph, who had a dream from God. But the wisdom of ensuring that food will be available in bad times has always been essential to survival. As you prepare this tasty winter chili, pray for all the people who brought it to your kitchen: checkout clerks, cannery workers, pickers, tractor operators, salt miners and onion packagers.

Vegetarian Chili

1 tbs. olive oil
1 bell pepper, chopped
2 onions, chopped
3 cloves garlic, finely
    chopped
2 carrots, diced
3 celery stalks, chopped
1 zucchini, halved and
    chopped
1 yellow summer squash,
    halved and chopped
2 28-oz. cans chopped
    tomatoes or
    5 lb. fresh tomatoes,
    chopped
2 tbs. chili powder
1 tsp. cumin
1 tsp. salt (optional)
2 cans black beans, drained
    and rinsed
2 cans pinto or kidney
    beans, drained and
    rinsed

Heat the oil in a large pot over medium heat. Add the bell pepper, onions and garlic. Sauté until the onion is soft (about 4 minutes). Add the remaining vegetables and seasoning. Simmer until the carrots are tender (about 15 minutes). Add the beans and simmer until heated through. *Serves 8.*

Every cook has to learn how to govern the state.

Vladimir Ilyich Lenin, from
Will the Bolsheviks Retain Government Power?

BE LEAVEN FOR THE KINGDOM

"The kingdom of heaven is like yeast that a woman took and mixed in with three measures of flour until all of it was leavened."—Matt. 13:33

Yeast is a living organism—a fungus. It can be "started" (by catching and feeding airborne amoebas) with flour, water, air and grapes to assist the fermentation process. The starter needs a constant temperature of about 75°, and feedings of flour and warm water three times a day—like a child. It keeps growing unless it is starved or the heat of the oven kills it. Yeasts that are decades old are very sturdy; they seem to have developed a resistance to bacteria, as if they carry their own strain of penicillin. A single mature starter or yeast will last a lifetime if it's cared for. Faith is like that starter. Once we receive it, it is our task to nurture and care for it.

Jesus says that the kingdom of God is like a well-fed, mature yeast—unstoppable. It will keep growing, leavening the world. This "kingdom starter" overtakes us, fermenting us and changing our nature, gracing us with life in God. Yet it is up to us to mix it in large measures, knead it and feed it. When I look at history's worst evils, I can't imagine how belief in God could ever overtake the greed and pride that cause such enormous human suffering. But when I look within myself, I know that God's love softens my own hard heart. The leaven of God's kingdom is strong enough to work in me. And my love is the food that nourishes the yeast, making it strong enough to work in others. Like yeast, our faith expands, permeating our life experiences and changing them from isolated events into a unified expression of our life in God.

Lent seems the right time to meditate on bread and bake some as well.

EAT OF THE LIVING BREAD

"I am the bread of life. Your ancestors ate the manna in the wilderness and they died. This is the bread that comes down from heaven, so that one may eat of it and not die. I am the living bread that came down from heaven. Whoever eats of this bread will live forever; and the bread that I will give for the life of the world is my flesh."—John 6:48-51

This scripture passage is the bread of the Christian faith, a staple in our pantry of belief. Jesus doesn't recant on this teaching. In John's sixth chapter, Jesus multiplies the loaves and fish, walks across the sea to the apostles in their boat, calms the sea, and then the next morning preaches to the multitude he'd fed the day before. When they ask for signs, he tells them that even manna in the desert wouldn't be enough for them. Then he says that he is living bread. Many of them walk away; he doesn't call them back.

That Jesus is living bread is an unfathomable mystery. Contemplating a living starter that leavens bread deepens my participation in that mystery. I've never made a starter, but one of these Lenten seasons I might, because it links the mystery to the mundane. For the moment I'll continue to contemplate making starter. If you decide to make your own, read a little more before you begin. I recommend *Breads from the La Brea Bakery* by Nancy Silverton.

How to Make a Starter

cheesecloth
rubber spatula (optional)
1-gallon plastic, ceramic or glass container
long-stemmed, instant-read cooking thermometer
room thermometer
1 lb. red or black grapes (pesticide free)
4 cups lukewarm water, 78°
3¼   cups unbleached white-bread flour

Clean everything so you don't contaminate the starter. Wash the grapes and put them on a double layer of cheesecloth. Tie the corners together to make a bag. Stir the water and flour together with your hands or a rubber spatula. Hold the grapes over the mixture and mash them, squeezing in the juice. Then swish the bag of grapes through the mixture a few times, push the bag to the bottom, and cover the container tightly. Leave it at room temperature, 70° to 75°. On days two and three, the mixture will bubble and begin to ferment.

On day four, refresh the culture: **1 cup lukewarm water, 78°**
                                           1 cup unbleached white flour
The mixture may be turning brownish purple and seething with large bubbles. A distinct, unpleasant, alcohol-like smell should be present. Add flour and water and mix with your hands or a rubber spatula. Be sure to swish the grape bag through the entire mixture and leave it in the mixture. Let the mixture sit tightly covered at room temperature for the next 5 days.

On day 10:   **One 6-quart plastic, ceramic or glass container, covered but not airtight**
Early in the day, open the mixture and remove the bag of grapes, squeezing any liquid back into your starter. Pour off and discard all but 2 cups of the culture. (Give the rest to friends or freeze it in case this batch fails.) Pick a regular schedule—three times a days, same times every day, at 4 to 6 hour intervals—to feed the starter. Double the starter with flour and water each time through day 15, pouring off all but 2 cups every morning.

> *1st feeding:* **1 cup lukewarm water, 1¹/₃ cups flour**
> *2nd feeding:* **2 cups lukewarm water, 3 cups flour**
> *3rd feeding:* **4 cups lukewarm water, 5½ cups flour**

On day 15, the starter is full-grown and you are ready to bake. (Remember, to keep the starter alive, feed it three times a day, continuously, according to the above directions.) For most recipes, 1 cup of starter replaces 1 package of yeast, ¹/₃ cup of water, and ²/₃ cup of flour.

THE SECRET OF FASTING

"And whenever you fast, do not look dismal, like the hypocrites, for they disfigure their faces so as to show others that they are fasting. Truly I tell you, they have received their reward. But when you fast, put oil on your head and wash your face, so that your fasting may be seen not by others but by your Father who is in secret; and your Father who sees in secret will reward you."
—Matt. 6:16-18

Fasting is an ancient spiritual practice. It's not a good weight-loss strategy. Our bodies will regain the lost pounds plus more in protection against the possibility of another famine. But judicious fasting (with its unbidden images of mashed potatoes caused by the mild sensory deprivation) always makes me laugh, even as it clears my mind of pride, envy, greed, lust, sloth, gluttony and anger. Although I tire more easily when I fast, I feel new energy and enthusiasm for life.

The simplest fasting, giving up sweets for Lent or going to bed hungry, is an opportunity to strengthen the muscles of our will without feeling superior to anybody. It's a little sacrifice. Going without for a few brief moments puts us in solidarity with people who have nothing and makes us appreciate all the more the pleasures of our bread and wine.

What should you cook when you're not having any? Cook something that smells good. Fasting sharpens all the other senses, so this is a good day to fill the house with a delightful aroma. In other words, a fast day is a good day to bake bread.

Plain White Bread

1 pkg. dry yeast
¼   cup very warm water
      (105° to 115°)
4½ cups unbleached
      all-purpose flour
1¼ tsp. salt
1¼ cups plus 2 tbs. water,
      room temperature

Combine the yeast and warm water in glass or cup. Let it stand for 3 minutes. Mix the flour and salt in large bowl. Add the yeasty water. Mix with your fingers, then slowly add 1¼ cups of room temperature water and knead on a lightly floured flat surface for about 4 minutes. Add additional tablespoons of water if needed.

Cover the dough with a cloth and let it stand for 20 minutes. Now knead it for 5 to 8 minutes, until it is smooth and elastic. Lightly dust a bowl with flour and put the dough in it. Cover again with a cloth and keep it at a warm room temperature, away from drafts, until it doubles in volume (about 2 hours).

Return the dough to a very lightly floured surface. Knead it again. Form loaves and place them in two lightly greased bread pans. Cover the loaves and allow them to rise again, doubling in size (less than 2 hours). Bake at 350° for 40 minutes or until the crust is brown, the bread has pulled away from the sides of the pan and a tap of the top of the bread sounds hollow. *Makes 2 loaves of bread.*

ALL IN A DAY'S WORK

When they found him on the other side of the sea, they said to him, "Rabbi, when did you come here?" Jesus answered them, "Very truly, I tell you, you are looking for me, not because you saw signs, but because you ate your fill of the loaves. Do not work for the food that perishes, but for the food that endures for eternal life, which the Son of Man will give you. For it is on him that God the Father has set his seal."—John 6:25-27

Baking bread with yeast reminds us that, even as cooks, we don't do all the work. We allow the dough to rise. We also need to allow God to work within us—to provide the food that endures for eternal life. My grandmother made bread for us at least once a week. She let me scrape out the leavings of dough from the mixing bowl to knead and form into the round balls for cloverleaf rolls. She was fond of telling the story about the Irish prince who posed as a beggar and asked for the scraps of dough and married the girl who said she had used up all her leavings but would be glad to give him a slice of fresh-baked bread.

My grandmother said the cloverleaf was in honor of Saint Patrick and to be mindful of the Trinity. She also kept a first-class relic of Saint Anthony (a piece of bone in a small glass case) in the bread box, relying on him to keep us in bread even as she baked. I realize now that she had a good grasp of the teaching that we should worry less and rely on God more. She was working for the food that endures for eternal life. Here is my grandmother's recipe for bread rolls.

CLOVERLEAF ROLLS

2 pkgs. dry yeast
1 cup warm water
2 cups milk
1 tbs. butter
1 tbs. sugar
1 tsp. salt

5 to 8 cups white flour, sifted

GLAZE
¼ cup water
3 tbs. granulated sugar

Dissolve the yeast in the cup of warm water. Scald the milk but don't let it boil. Remove it from the heat and add the butter, sugar and salt. Let the milk stand until the butter melts. Then mix in the yeasty water.

In a large bowl, stir the liquid into the flour. When the mixture changes into dough, turn it onto a flat, floured surface and knead it with your hands. Add more flour until dough is smooth and elastic and no longer sticks to the table or your hands (probably 7 cups in all, depending on temperature and humidity). Be careful not to add too much flour or the bread will be tough.

Return the dough to its bowl and set it in a warm corner, covered, away from drafts to double in size (about an hour). Knead the dough on a floured surface and let it rise again, about another hour. Punch the dough down on a very lightly floured surface once more and then form rolls. Grease the muffin tins and, to keep the dough from sticking to your fingers, this time you may oil your hands lightly. Make the cloverleaf rolls by forming golf ball pieces of dough and placing them in groups of three in muffin tins. Cover the formed rolls and place them back in a warm corner to rise again for 30 to 60 minutes.

Place the rolls in the oven at 425° for 5 minutes, then reduce the heat to 350°. Bake for 20 minutes more or until the tops are golden brown, the sides have pulled away from the tin and taps on the tops sound hollow. Tip the rolls in the muffin tins so the bread bottom doesn't sweat and get soggy or cool the rolls on a wire rack. If a glaze is desired, brush the hot tops with mix of ¼ cup water and 3 tbs. sugar. *Makes 48 rolls (or 4 loaves of bread, if you prefer).*

Hope is the poor person's bread.

GEORGE HERBERT

THE BAKER'S DISCIPLINE

"Give us this day our daily bread."—Matt. 6:11

Bread is ordinary. We eat it every day. But as we've seen, it takes skill to bake it—patience, care of the yeast, and feel for consistency of the dough. Think of what we're asking our Father for when we pray the Lord's prayer. We're asking for the work of God's hands to become the work of human hands.

It takes time and attention to make bread. That's why most of us seldom do it—unless we have a bread machine. A bread machine is a great invention—it makes it easy to fill the house with a wonderful aroma. When I was little, my father took any of us who went to daily Mass with him to the bakery afterwards to pick out sweet rolls for the family. He'd say, "Smell that fresh bread. It's the best smell in the world." I chided him once that he was bribing us to go to Mass. "No," he said. "Everybody gets sweet rolls, whether you come to Mass or not. But all your lives, when you walk into a bakery, you will make a pleasant association with going to church."

Perhaps you and I, working through these meditations, will think of Jesus every time we smell fresh bread.

USING A BREAD MACHINE

I don't have a true recipe for a bread machine, only a warning: follow the directions. Follow them exactly, because the baking process by hand and by machine differs. The discipline of baking bread by hand is dictated by the bread. It reacts to humidity, temperature, kneading and the quality of heat in the oven. The baker learns to adjust times and ingredients slightly in response to the feel of the dough. The discipline of the machine leaves no room for intuitive judgments. The baker must read the instructions and obey them.

The first five books of scripture, the Torah, is a sort of bread machine for living in community. Israel's law at its best eliminates worry about intuiting what is good or bad. This was crucial to Hebrew life in God because, for the first time in recorded history, the behavior of the *people* had spiritual significance. Prior to Israel, only the behavior of the *king* shaped a nation's religious life. Now every deed of every Jew counted. The laws of the Torah meant that Jews didn't have to define godly behavior for themselves. Their reward for obeying the law was confidence that they were truly participating in the life of God. Obeying the bread machine's instructions grants us a more mundane reward: fresh-baked bread. But if we choose to pay attention, we can turn even this baking tool into a reminder of God.

This food reveals our connection with the Earth. Each bite contains the life of the sun and the Earth. The extent to which our food reveals itself depends on us. We can see and taste the whole universe in a piece of bread.

THICH NHAT HANH, from *Present Moment, Wonderful Moment*

BREAD BUILDS STRONG BODIES

You cause the grass to grow for the cattle,
and plants for people to use,
to bring forth food from the earth
and wine to gladden the human heart,
oil to make the face shine,
and bread to strengthen the human heart.
—Psalm 104:14-15

Good bread does strengthen the human heart—and the body as well. Most everybody eats some kind of bread every day. It used to be brown or creamy white and chewy with fiber, baked locally. But industrialized city bakeries have become reliant on refined white flour, trucked in from huge industrial mills. Grocery chains like plastic-wrapped, symmetrical, snow-white loaves that slice and stack neatly and are laden with preservatives. That these loaves have little flavor or substance matters less to consumers than that they're cheap. Some consumers, having grown up on processed white bread, have learned to like it best.

Refining white flour takes out the fiber our digestive systems need. So now the more expensive bakeries and store-bought brands have put the fiber back into bread. For the home baker, these grains are costly and hard to store, and the family may not like them. But it's always good to have a recipe on hand.

Multigrain Bread

1 cup water
1 cup plain yogurt
¼ cup vegetable oil
½ cup oats
⅓ cup wheat germ
⅓ cup unprocessed bran
5 to 5½ cups all-purpose
    flour
¼ cup light brown sugar,
    firmly packed
2 pkgs. dry yeast
2 tsp. salt
2 eggs

Heat the water, yogurt and vegetable oil to simmering. Stir in the oats, wheat germ and bran. Let the mixture stand for about 30 minutes at room temperature.

In a large bowl mix 1 cup of flour with the sugar, dry yeast and salt. Add the cool bran mix and blend well. Stir in 1 egg and the remaining flour. Knead the dough until it is supple, 6 to 8 minutes. Place it back in the mixing bowl, cover it, place it away from drafts and let it rise for 10 minutes.

Knead it down, divide it into two loaves and place them in loaf pans. Let them rise 30 to 40 minutes. Across the top of each loaf make three diagonal slashes with a sharp knife. Beat the remaining egg and brush it on the loaf tops. Sprinkle oats or wheat germ on the loaf tops. Bake at 375° for 25 to 30 minutes, or until bread is brown and taps on the tops sound hollow. Cool bread on wire racks.˘

God is bread when you're hungry, water when you're thirsty,
a harbor from the storm.

Bear (Lakota), from *In the Spirit of Crazy Horse*
by Peter Matthiesson

GIVE THANKS

"We remember the fish we used to eat in Egypt for nothing, the cucumbers, the melons, the leeks, the onions and the garlic; but now our strength is dried up, and there is nothing at all but this manna to look at."

Now the manna was like coriander seed, and its color was like the color of gum resin. The people went around and gathered it, ground it in mills or beat it in mortars, then boiled it in pots and made cakes of it; and the taste of it was like the taste of cakes baked with oil. When the dew fell on the camp in the night, the manna would fall with it.—Num. 11:5-9

Every morning in the desert the manna lay everywhere. Eventually, the Israelites tired of manna and began to complain about it. They forgot to give thanks. Manna prefigures the Eucharist, which means "thanksgiving." Sharing the Eucharist is an act of thanksgiving for life, for salvation, for family and community, and for the food itself. Moments of gratitude are moments of great grace. But it's easy to get bored and forget to give thanks.

The Catholic Worker shelter where I do some work used to get terrific leftover pizza from one of the franchises. Today pizza, like manna, is everywhere. You can find it in pizza parlors, specialty shops, supermarket delis and the frozen-food section of supermarkets. Like the ancient Israelites, the homeless guests and the Worker community got bored with pizza. We began to complain. Then the franchise stopped giving us pizza, and that, too, caused complaints.

We humans need variety in our lives; at the same time, we are reluctant to try out new ideas. Still and all, it gives me a chuckle to see all that pizza in the freezer bins at the grocery and remember the manna in the desert. Pizza's become a little reminder to me that God provides.

Why bother to make it at home? Because it's easy, inexpensive and superb.

Pizza Crust

1 pkg. dry yeast
¼ cup warm water
3 cups flour
1 tsp. salt
2 tbs. olive oil
1 tbs. honey
¾ cup water, room
     temperature

OPTIONAL ADDITIONS
TO THE KNEADED DOUGH

¼ cup chopped olives or
1 clove minced garlic or
2 tbs. chopped fresh basil or
¼ tsp. red pepper flakes and
¼ cup parmesan cheese or
¼ cup romano cheese

TOPPING
See p. 15 for pizza topping,
or top with **cheese, tomato
sauce, vegetables,** and /or
cooked meat.

Dissolve the yeast in warm water in a glass or ceramic cup; let it stand 10 minutes.

Combine the flour, salt, oil, honey and room temperature water in a large bowl. Add the dissolved yeast, stir to blend. Knead by hand until smooth.

Add any optional ingredients to the dough. Don't overwhelm the dough with flavors.

Form the dough into a ball and place it in an oiled bowl. Turn the dough to coat its entire surface with oil. Cover with a towel and set in a warm place until doubled in bulk, at least 60 minutes.

Punch the dough down and knead it briefly. Use your hands or a rolling pin to form the crust on a lightly oiled pizza pan. Prebake the crust for 10 minutes at 450°. Then add topping and cook until cheese bubbles, or freeze for future use. *Makes 1 large or 2 medium pizza crusts.*

DISTRIBUTE THE PLENTY

When he looked up and saw a large crowd coming toward him, Jesus said to Philip, "Where are we to buy bread for these people to eat?" He said this to test him, for he himself knew what he was going to do. Philip answered him, "Six months' wages would not buy enough bread for each of them to get a little." One of his disciples, Andrew, Simon Peter's brother, said to him, "There is a boy here who has five barley loaves and two fish. But what are they among so many people?" Jesus said, "Make the people sit down." Now there was a great deal of grass in the place; so they sat down, about five thousand in all. Then Jesus took the loaves, and when he had given thanks, he distributed them to those who were seated; so also the fish, as much as they wanted. When they were satisfied, he told his disciples, "Gather up the fragments left over, so that nothing may be lost."—John 6:5-14

"So that nothing may be lost." How little do we heed those words. Hunger is increasing in the world. The wealthy 10 percent eat expensive corn-fed beef as fast food while half the world goes to bed hungry and 12 million children under 5 die each year, mainly from preventable diseases and malnutrition.

The poorest lay waste their land by burning the rain forest for fuel, and thus cause erosion, reduce rainfall and warm the atmosphere. The rich warm the atmosphere even more by burning fossil fuels. The poor are thin, the rich are fat.

The so-called farming miracles—fertilizers, pesticides and hybrid seeds—are polluting rivers, poisoning animals and people, and extinguishing the genetic variation in crops. This is *problematic* in the great corn and wheat belts, where millions of acres of the same genetically engineered, hybrid seed may prove vulnerable to mutant pests and viruses that are immune to pesticides. But it is a *crisis* in regions where farmers have run out of funds to purchase that hybrid seed along with the fertilizer and pesticides it demands. Meanwhile, many of the open-pollination seeds—the seeds our grandparents used—have been lost.

It would be a great miracle for us, the rich, to choose to live on less. We'd share our excess grain instead of feeding it to cattle. We'd pay more for chicken instead of converting more black bean fields to sorghum for chicken feed. We'd cease demanding exotic cash crops like pineapple and carnations. Our restraint today would free more resources for the poor and protect the land for our children's children for generations to come.

Irish Soda Bread

2 cups flour
¹/₃ cup sugar
½ tsp. salt
1½ tsp. baking powder
½ tsp. baking soda
¾ cup raisins
1 tsp. caraway seeds
1 egg, lightly beaten
²/₃ cup buttermilk
1 tbs. butter, melted

Sift together the flour, sugar, salt, baking powder and soda. Add the raisins and caraway seeds. In a separate bowl, beat the egg and add the buttermilk and butter. Stir this into the dry ingredients. It should be just enough liquid to moisten the mixture throughout. If the dough is too sticky to handle, add a little flour. (Usually it needs more, but be careful not to add too much.) Knead lightly with your hands and shape it into a plump disk. Cut a cross on top of the bread, place it on a greased cookie sheet, and bake in at 350° for 30 to 35 minutes.

Russian Soda Bread

Replace the raisins and caraway seeds above with **½ tsp. saffron** and **a half shot of brandy**.

Italian Soda Bread

Replace the raisins and caraway seeds above with **grated lemon rind, anise, candied fruit, pine nuts** and **an extra egg yolk**.

Norwegian Julekaka

Replace the caraway seeds above with **1 tsp. cardamom** and add **citron**.

TASTE AND SEE

While they were eating, Jesus took bread, gave thanks and broke it, and gave it to his disciples saying, "Take and eat; this is my body."—Matt. 26:26

Bread is the universal food—whether it be white, wheat, sour dough, potato bread or matzoth, bagels, rice cakes, pancakes, buns, biscuits, tortillas, or muffins. We find it everywhere—whether the flour comes from wheat, corn, potatoes, rice, oats or soybeans; and whether it's fried, baked, or boiled, it's still bread.

Eating bread makes us one body, poor and rich, believers and nonbelievers, Asians and Africans, Europeans and Americans, young and old. Whatever land we visit, we can break bread with the people. Bread crosses all the boundaries we have set up among us.

That's why Jesus chose bread as the medium to maintain his physical presence among us. Psalm 34:8 says, "O taste and see that the Lord is good." Taste different breads. Taste different cultures. See how good the Lord is.

Corn Tortillas

1 pkg. masa
add water as directed on
      package

Shape the tortillas by patting them out. Place them on a dry hot skillet. Flip when the edges are dry. Tortillas are simple to make, but not easy. It takes practice to shape these flat round breads.

. . . Eating is an activity that joins me with all humanity. I recognize that to be an eater is to be accountable for the care of the earth and its resources. I acknowledge that despite our differences, we are all ultimately nourished by the same source. As such, I agree to share.

I recognize that at its deepest level eating is an affirmation of life. Each time I eat I agree somewhere inside to continue life on earth. I acknowledge that this choice to eat is a fundamental act of love and nourishment, a true celebration of my existence. As a human being on earth, I agree to be an eater. I choose life again and again and again.

Marc David, from *Nourishing Wisdom*

POWER PLAYS

The tempter came and said to him, "If you are the Son of God, command these stones to become loaves of bread." But he answered, "It is written, 'One does not live by bread alone, but by every word that comes from the mouth of God.'"—Matt. 4:3-4

Christ's temptation was about power, not about feeding the hungry. The tempter wants Jesus to use his power to claim recognition and authority in the world, feeding his own hunger and others only incidentally. This temptation is like one nation's embargo on wheat shipments to force another nation to behave differently. The method is a brute display of power.

Jesus rejected power as a tool for changing our hearts. He chose the word of God. And he chose bread as his instrument of communion with us and thanksgiving to God. But he left us the task of making (or buying) the bread and putting it on the table. Below is a recipe for tasty breakfast muffins that pack enough power to get us through the morning's work to lunch time.

MUFFINS WITH OATMEAL, WALNUTS AND DATES

1 cup oatmeal
1 cup buttermilk
1 egg, beaten
1/3 cup brown sugar
1/2 cup vegetable oil
  or 1 tbs. oil and 1/2 cup
  applesauce
1/2 cup whole-wheat flour
1/2 cup white flour
1 tsp. baking powder
1/2 tsp. salt
1/2 tsp. baking soda
1/2 cup dates, chopped
1/2 cup walnuts, chopped
1/4 cup wheat germ
  (optional)

Mix all the ingredients together, spoon them into greased muffin tins and bake at 400° for 20 minutes or until a toothpick inserted into the center comes out clean. *Makes 24 muffins.*

Lenten fasting is not the same thing in those lands where people eat well as is a Lent among our third world peoples, undernourished as they are, living in a perpetual Lent, always fasting. For those who eat well, Lent is a call to austerity, a call to give away in order to share with those in need. But in poor lands, in homes where there is hunger, Lent should be observed in order to give to the sacrifice that is everyday life the meaning of the cross.

OSCAR ROMERO

ONE BREAD, ONE BODY

The cup of blessing that we bless, is it not a sharing in the blood of Christ? The bread that we break, is it not a sharing in the body of Christ? Because there is one bread, we who are many are one body, for we all partake of the one bread.—I Cor. 10:16-17

What does it mean to say that we are one body? Spouses join together in an act of love. Children are born from our bodies. But, day to day, we perceive even those we love most as different from us. Yet humans inherently long for union. At our best we look at people of different gender, personality, culture or skin color and wish we could transcend the differences. We imagine walking in other moccasins. And at the same time we are terrified of losing our individuality. We hold on to what makes us different—so stubbornly that we sometimes pick fights with those we love the most.

How do we let Jesus' words take us into the deeper truth of universal fellowship? By the simple practice of mindfulness: remembering Jesus. When he broke bread at the Last Supper, he told us to imitate his action so as to remember him. If every time we break bread we remember Jesus and his command to love, then—mouthful by mouthful of bread—we will move, over our lifetime, toward that deeper mystical union that is ours to claim for all eternity.

Bread is so common, we are so small and our vision is so grand. Clearly, in our desire to be one we are engaged in divine foolishness. Let these unusual cheese muffins remind us of our deepest hopes and desires.

Honey Bran Muffins with Cheddar Cheese

¾ **cup white flour**
½ **cup wheat flour**
1 cup unprocessed wheat
    bran or wheat germ
1 tbs. baking powder
¼ **tsp. baking soda**
pinch of salt
1 cup buttermilk
⅓ **cup honey**
6 tbs. butter, melted
1 large egg
¼ **tsp. vanilla**
1 cup sharp cheddar cheese,
    shredded

Combine the first six ingredients in a large bowl.

In a separate bowl, whisk the buttermilk, honey, butter, egg and vanilla.

Combine mixture with the dry ingredients, and then fold in the cheese. Pour into lightly greased muffin tins and bake at 400° for 20 minutes or until a toothpick inserted in the center comes out clean. *Makes 24 muffins.*

Be gentle when you touch bread.
Let it not lie uncared for,
Unwanted.
So often bread is taken for granted.
There is such beauty in bread—
Beauty of surf and soil,
Beauty of patient toil.
Wind and rain have caressed it,
Christ often blessed it.
Be gentle when you touch bread.
CELTIC PRAYER, from *The Open Gate*
by David Adam

COMMUNITY BUILDING

They devoted themselves to the apostles' teaching and fellowship, to the breaking of bread and the prayers. Awe came upon everyone, because many wonders and signs were being done by the apostles.—Acts 2:42-43

There is a Guinness world record for the fastest loaf of bread ever baked. It's held by the Wheat Montana Farms and Bakery. The bakery set up a tent next to a stand of ripened wheat, parked a reaper at the far end of the row, ran electricity out to the tent and stocked the tent with mill, scales, mixer, microwave ovens, greased pans, water, salt and yeast. The clock started when the reaper started. The baker mixed the yeast with water and turned on the mill. The fresh-cut wheat was run to the tent, milled, weighed and dumped into the mixer with the salt and the yeasty water. From the mixer it went into thirteen baking pans and then into thirteen microwave ovens with only seconds of baking time to rise before the heat killed the yeast. But the Guinness judges deemed it bread, made from harvest to first bite in 19 minutes, 45 seconds.

I started this series of Lenten bread-baking reflections by stressing the slow growth of the leaven and the baker's patient attentiveness. But even this most contemplative of kitchen tasks, central to Christian life since the days of the first Christian communities, has become an event for the record books. Which just goes to show that bread baking can be awesome in more ways than one!

FAST BUTTERMILK YEAST ROLLS

1¼ **cups buttermilk**
¼ **cup water**
1 tbs. butter
½ **cup rolled oats**
2½ **cups all-purpose flour**
2 pkgs. dry yeast
1 tbs. sugar
1 tsp. salt
½ **tsp. baking soda**
butter for baking sheet

Heat the buttermilk, water and butter together until the butter is melted. Remove the mixture from the heat. Pour the oats into a large bowl and sift in the remaining dry ingredients. Add the warm liquid and stir.

Place the dough onto a floured board and knead it gently for about 5 minutes, working in more flour as needed. Divide the dough into 12 equal pieces by cutting it in half, half again, and then thirds.

Lightly butter your hands and shape each piece into a ball. Arrange the balls on a buttered baking sheet and cover with a towel. Cover the rolls and place the baking sheet in a warm corner and allow the rolls to rise for an hour. Bake at 350° for 20 minutes or until the rolls are lightly browned and sound hollow when the tops are tapped. Cool on rack. *Makes 1 dozen rolls.*

PASSOVER, HOLY THURSDAY:
CHOSEN FOR LOVE

On the first day of Unleavened Bread the disciples came to Jesus, saying, "Where do you want us to make the preparations for you to eat the Passover?" He said, "Go into the city to a certain man, and say to him, 'The Teacher says, My time is near; I will keep the Passover at your house with my disciples.'" So the disciples did as Jesus had directed them, and they prepared the Passover meal.—Matt. 26:17-19

Holy Thursday is a night of contradictions. In Jewish and Christian tradition the night of Passover is a night unlike any other because it marks us as God's own people. It is a night to gather the family around, serve a fine meal, and rejoice in one another. For Christians, it is also the night of Jesus' Last Supper: the night he gave us the Eucharist, washed his apostles' feet, suffered agony in the Garden of Gethsemane, and was betrayed by Judas and denied by Peter.

Our love for the faces gathered around our Passover table makes us fear the dangers outside our home. That love also enhances our joy in what the future holds for our family and our gratitude for their presence. The Lenten season magnifies our fears and hopes, our pain and gratitude through the lens of Jesus' journey and resolves them through our faith that with God all shall be well.

So whether this has been a year of sorrow or joy, Holy Thursday dinner should celebrate our belief that we are God's people. It offers us a moment of pause in our hurried pace to remember that God has chosen to save us, to free us from our sins and protect us from all anxieties.

If you wish to serve a simple Passover meal, the menu includes lamb, a salad of bitter herbs (radishes, endive, spinach, dandelion greens), unleavened bread (crackers or matzoth), a sweet sauce of apples and raisins and wine or grape juice. On this night of contradictions I've gone outside the boundaries of Lenten bread recipes to include one for leg of lamb.

Leg of Lamb

1 leg of lamb
20 cloves of garlic
20 sprigs of rosemary
20 thin slices of prosciutto
1 cup sherry

Make 20 packets of garlic and rosemary, wrapped in prosciutto

Spear the lamb about 20 times. Into each gash push a garlic-rosemary-prosciutto packet. Roast the lamb, uncovered or on a rack, in a very hot oven (475°) for 15 minutes. Reduce the heat to 350°. Allow 20 minutes per pound to reach an internal temperature of 175° to 180°. Baste with sherry a half hour before lamb is done.

When we cast our bread upon the waters, we can presume that someone downstream whose face we will never know will benefit from our action, as we who are downstream from another will profit from that grantor's gift.

Maya Angelou

GOOD FRIDAY:
WE KNOW NOT WHAT WE DO

Then Jesus cried again with a loud voice and breathed his last. At that moment the curtain of the temple was torn in two, from top to bottom. The earth shook, and the rocks were split.—Matt. 27:50-51

Why in some cultures is Good Friday marked by hot cross buns, a sweet bread? I think because it is a comfort food. The cross, of course, is a memorial, and the sweetness is a reminder of Easter joy. The scent of hot bread baking, filling the house on Good Friday morning, comforts the whole family and reminds us that we are safe within the saving act of redemption.

Meanwhile, hundreds of men and women sit on death row across the United States, awaiting their deaths at the hand of the state. Some people are too bent by evil or by illness ever to be allowed free, but killing them diminishes us. There are many arguments against the death penalty: that some who are innocent, like Jesus, will be killed; that the poor are disproportionately represented; that capital punishment does not deter crime. When our government kills a person in our names—no matter how heinous the crime committed—we become less human. The earth shakes, rocks split, because we've decreased our participation in the life of God.

Pray for these men and women on death row. Work to end the death penalty because our lives in God are linked to theirs.

Hot Cross Buns

2 pkgs. dry yeast	4½ cups flour
½ cup warm water	
½ cup milk, scalded	Frosting
½ cup sugar	1 cup powdered sugar
1 tsp. salt	1 tbs. butter
½ cup margarine	½ tsp. vanilla
2 eggs, beaten	1 tsp. lemon juice
1 tbs. grated lemon rind	2 tbs. milk or lemon yogurt

Mix the yeast and warm water. Let it stand for 15 minutes. Mix the milk, sugar, salt and margarine. Allow to cool to 110° (cool enough to keep your finger in the liquid until the count of ten.) Add the eggs and grated lemon rind. Add the yeast mixture. Gradually stir the flour into the center of the liquid. As the mixture becomes stiff, use your hands to work it into dough. Knead the dough until it's smooth. Cover it and set it in a warm place to rise for about an hour. Knead it down again. Kneading will give the bread texture, but too much kneading (and too much flour) will make it tough.

Let the dough rise again. Punch it down once more. Divide into 12 equal pieces, shape the dough into balls and place them in greased muffin tins. If you wish, take a golf ball-sized piece of dough, add two drops of yellow food coloring, and place a bit of colored dough in the center of each roll (to simulate an egg yolk). With a scissors, cut a cross into the top of each roll. Cover the rolls and allow them to rise one more time. Bake them in a 350° oven for 30 to 40 minutes, until the crust is brown, the dough has pulled away from the sides of the pan and a tap on the top of the rolls makes a hollow sound. Cool buns on a rack or tip them on their sides in the pan.

Mix the frosting ingredients in a small bowl and apply frosting in the form of a cross on each roll. *Makes 1 dozen buns.*

HOLY SATURDAY:
QUIET PREPARATION

The women who had come with him from Galilee followed, and they saw the tomb and how his body was laid. Then they returned, and prepared spices and ointments. On the Sabbath they rested according to the commandment.
—Luke 25:55-56

Exhaustion sets in the day following the death of a loved one. When one is drained physically and emotionally, simple tasks take overwhelming effort. As you go about your routine on Holy Saturday, keep your movements spare and quiet. Take time to ponder the mysteries of Christ's life and death.

Eggs are a symbol of the Resurrection. Prepare for Easter by decorating eggs with children (or for your own pleasure) and think about those eggs. They promise new life—and thus hope. The cheap, common, ordinary egg stands for potential. So make it beautiful.

Hard-Boiled Eggs

Put the eggs in cold water and bring it to a boil. Boil the eggs for 12 minutes. Immediately remove them from the stove and run the eggs under cold water. This will make them easier to peel and keep the edges of the yolks from discoloring before you finally do eat them.

A simple decorating trick for children is to draw or write their names on the eggs in white crayon before dipping them in Easter-egg dye.

A simple cooking trick for adults, since one egg contains as much cholesterol as an adult should eat in a day: use one whole egg and one additional egg white whenever a recipe calls for two eggs. Cook the other yolk and feed it to an animal.

All the qualities of a spiritual teacher can be found in a person who can cook an egg perfectly.

Sufi teacher, as quoted in *Spiritual Literacy*
by Frederick and Mary Ann Brussat

EASTER:
RECOGNIZING GOD AMONG US

When he was at the table with them, he took bread, blessed and broke it, and gave it to them. Then their eyes were opened, and they recognized him; and he vanished from their sight. They said to each other, "Were not our hearts burning within us while he was talking to us on the road, while he was opening the scriptures to us?" That same hour they got up and returned to Jerusalem; and they found the eleven and their companions gathered together. They were saying, "The Lord has risen indeed, and he has appeared to Simon." Then they told what had happened on the road, and how he had been made known to them in the breaking of the bread.—Luke 24:30-35

Often we avert our eyes to avoid a moment of recognition. We don't want to face a beggar at the door of a department store or a street person washing our windshield at a traffic light. We don't want to look at refugees or crippled children or people racked with pain and disease. We shy away from strangers on a plane and worshipers who share our pew in church. But sometimes we look. And once in a while, when we look, we recognize the Lord. Each recognition is a small Easter in us—"a daystar to the dimness," as Gerard Manley Hopkins said. Perhaps the more bread each one of us breaks, the better we'll recognize the Lord in the breaking.

Challah is the Jewish bread for celebration of the Sabbath. It's a wonderful light, white bread. Serve it whole and let everyone tear off his or her portion, the better to remember our community in Jesus.

CHALLAH BREAD

5 cups flour
2 pkgs. dry yeast
1 tsp. salt
⅔ cup sugar
¼ cup margarine or butter
1½ cups very hot water (130°)
2 eggs, well beaten

TOPPING
1 egg, beaten
sesame or poppy seeds

Mix the dry ingredients, including the yeast in a large bowl. Melt the butter and mix it with water and the beaten eggs, then add the liquid to the dry mixture and stir until it's doughy. Knead the dough on a floured board for 10 minutes. (You will probably need to add more flour as you knead.)

Set the dough in a warm corner covered with a towel to double in size (about an hour). Punch down the dough and divide it into 3 pieces (or 6 pieces if you wish to make 2 loaves). Roll the pieces into ropes, braid them together, and place them on a greased baking sheet. Cover with a towel and let the loaves rise another hour.

Glaze with the beaten egg and top with seeds. Bake for 30 to 35 minutes at 350° or until the bread is golden and gives a hollow sound when tapped on the top. *Makes 1 large or 2 small loaves of bread.*

Spring: Ordinary Time

THE EYE OF THE BEHOLDER

Out of the ground the Lord God made to grow every tree that is pleasant to the sight and good for food.—Gen. 2:9

The Lord God also made dandelions. A long cool spring is great for dandelions. Their flower heads become enormous, their roots grow deep, and their seeds float on June winds across our lawns. To the eye accustomed to putting greens and manicured gardens, dandelions give the landscape a ragged look. They look ugly, and we want to dig them out.

But dandelions are a great food—all parts can be eaten. Young leaves, gathered before the flower forms, are the most tender and least bitter. Cultivated dandelions are tastier than wild ones, but even the weediest can be tossed in a salad or boiled like spinach. Try peeling the roots and adding them raw to a salad or throw them on the grill or in a frying pan. Dry and grind the roots, like chicory, for ersatz coffee. Munch on the yellow blossoms as you pick them, deep-fry them, mix them into pancake batter, or make wine. Dry the leaves for tea.

A half cup of uncooked dandelion leaves contains 280 percent of the adult daily requirement of beta carotene, half the vitamin C requirement, plus magnesium, calcium, iron and potassium.

Alas, dandelions are not pleasant to our adult sight. But six children I know under age 4 love to pick dandelions, eat their flowers and make a wish before blowing the fluffy seed carriers into the wind. My knowledge of the dandelion's usefulness makes me marvel all the more at God's bounty and human resourcefulness. I want to taste the flowers as well as smell them.

God lives in the details of our lives. This least of flowers, scorned and rejected, has the power to lift our hearts and minds to God as well as heal and feed us. Contemplate the dandelion this spring and rejoice in it—even while you're rooting it out of your lawn.

THE GOOD EARTH

But I have said to you: you shall inherit their land, and I will give it to you to possess, a land flowing with milk and honey. I am the Lord your God; I have separated you from the peoples.—Lev. 20:24

The expression "milk and honey" is the biblical metaphor for the good life. Plentiful cows' milk and hives of healthy bees pollinating crops and making delicious honey—these are still signs of the good life, indicating fertile land, enough rain and enough sun. No matter how advanced our technologies, cities and towns still depend on productive farmland. If our fields and cows stopped producing, civilization would dry up. God's Promised Land is, indeed, the land itself—the rich earth, which provides us with our daily sustenance.

I'm told that the secret of Mexican cooking is milk. Add a little to your refried beans. Pour a glassful to cut the fire of a jalapeño and be grateful for the cows and bees and our land of milk and honey.

CHILI RELLENOS

1 can (1 lb. 10 oz.) whole green mild chilis (or 6 4-oz. cans)
1 lb. chicken or turkey, ground
2 cups Monterey Jack or Mozzarella cheese, shredded,
4 eggs, beaten
1½ cups milk
¼ cup flour
1 tsp. salt
Tabasco sauce

Brown the meat. Grease a 13-by-9-inch pan, and line the bottom of the pan with some of the chilis. Alternate layers of meat, cheese and chilis until all the ingredients are used. In a separate bowl, mix the eggs, milk, flour, salt and Tabasco (to taste). Then pour the mixture over the casserole. Bake at 350° for 45 minutes, or until the mixture is set. *Serves 6.*

We aim at something more sublime and more equitable—the common good, or the community of goods. . . . We demand, we would have, the communal enjoyment of the fruits of the earth, fruits which are for everyone.

FRANÇOIS-NOËL BABEUF (GRACCHUS), from *Manifesto of the Equals*

RAIN WITH JUSTICE

A ruler who oppresses the poor is a beating rain that leaves no food.—Prov. 28:3

Imagine a driving rainstorm that knocks unripened fruit off the trees, batters the corn to the ground and washes the soil away from crop roots. We've all witnessed flash floods, at least on television, and know the damage they can do. Proverbs tells us that when we oppress the poor, we are like that beating rain.

It's easy to oppress the poor. They have few resources to stave off an attack or make known to the world the injustices being done to them. Often we are unaware of our own oppressiveness. We may give in charity and wonder what more we can do. What we can do is act with justice. Justice isn't the impulsively written check but the vote to improve schools, even if it means higher taxes; the support of fair housing, despite fears for our own property values; the recruitment of a diverse workforce, regardless of the extra effort it may take; the payment of a living wage, even if it means less profit. Our obligation is to shape our lives justly, using no more than our share of resources and actively seeking equity for others.

When we give generously and act justly, we are like the gentle spring rain that yields tender carrots, asparagus, onions and peas that are a perfect accompaniment to pasta.

Pasta Primavera (springtime vegetables and pasta)

1 lb. pasta (any will do)
3 tbs. olive oil
3 cloves garlic, minced
3 thin slices fresh ginger
1 medium onion, diced
4 carrots, chopped
2 cups cauliflower, chopped
2 cups broccoli
1 15-oz. can corn
1 cup snow or sugar snap
peas
(other favorite vegetables
may be added or
substituted)

Sauce
1 tbs. butter or margarine
1 tbs. cornstarch
½ cup milk
2 cups of cottage cheese
lemon pepper

For a lighter meal:
omit the sauce and add
8 oz. cubed cream cheese
lemon pepper

Add pasta to boiling water. Cook *al dente* (until tender but slightly chewy). Drain.

Heat the olive oil in a large skillet. Sauté the fresh vegetables starting with those that need the longest cooking time (as in the list to the left).

In a sauce pan, heat the butter. Add the cornstarch. Slowly add the cold milk, stirring constantly, to allow the sauce to thicken (about 3 minutes). Then add the cottage cheese.

Mix the pasta, vegetables and sauce. If the lighter version is chosen, simply mix the cubed cream cheese into the vegetables. Add pepper. *Serves 6.*

CAST A WIDE NET

"And I will make you fishers of men."—Matt. 4:18

Many of the apostles made their living by fishing—until Jesus called them to be fishers of men. They appeared to be nothing special. Each of us, one soul among 6 billion, appears to be nothing special. But we have been called by Jesus to live with him. He has made us apostles, too, fishers of souls. Jesus has given us the task of inviting our children's friends, our colleagues at work and our neighbors down the street to share in the vision of God's realm.

Jesus gave the apostles the courage to proclaim a new vision of life. That's our job, too. We have a redemptive role. It makes a difference that each one of us treats others well, opposes injustice and tells the truth.

Cooking fish, especially catfish, that most common of river creatures, is as good a time as any to examine our lives. Have we learned from Jesus how to draw others into the net of love for one another?

FRIED CATFISH

2 lbs. catfish fillets
1 cup yellow cornmeal
1 cup whole wheat flour
1 tsp. salt
1 tsp. pepper
1 tsp. poultry seasoning
8 cups vegetable oil

Place filets on a cutting board, skin side down. Starting from the large end of each filet, cut strips no more than ½ -inch wide. Mix the breading ingredients. Heat the oil in a deep fry pan or Dutch oven to 350°.

When the oil is hot, dip a dozen filets into the breading and drop them into the oil. (The oil will spatter vigorously.) Fry the fish for 3 to 5 minutes, depending on your taste. *Serves 6.*

They let themselves be caught by him. . . . That was the miraculous catch and not the haddock and shad and mojarras and all the other different fish they caught with the net. And they caught us and that's why we're gathered here.

ERNESTO CARDENAL, from *The Gospel in Solentiname*

BE LIKE LITTLE CHILDREN

"There is a boy here who has five barley loaves and two fish. But what are they among so many people?"—John 6:8-9

Who was this boy who gave away his loaves and fishes? He was probably on his way home with the groceries, but he got caught up, as young people get caught up, in the ideals Jesus offered. The boy thought, "Yes, this is right!" and offered his heart and his family's food.

We were like that when we were young. Swept up by high ideals, willing to make sacrifices and be open to the words of prophets. Now we may feel some irritation when we see that idealism in our children—when they're working for a cause while at home dishes go unwashed and beds unmade.

What happened to the boy? Was he punished for coming home late and empty-handed, or did Andrew, the apostle who brought him to Jesus' attention, remember to give him back his loaves and fishes from the 12 baskets leftover? Did his parents ask what kept him and then listen in wonder to his recounting of Jesus' teachings?

As you prepare dinner, think about what arouses idealism in children. Can you get your own children talking about what's important to them tonight at the supper table? Can you recapture some of your own youthful idealism?

BAKED SALMON WITH TOMATO-BASIL SAUCE

4 4-oz. salmon fillets
4 pats of butter
½ cup white wine
1 lemon

SAUCE
2 tomatoes
8 basil leaves or 1 tbs.
dry basil
1 tsp. parsley, chopped
cracked pepper
cayenne pepper to taste
¼ cup olive oil
½ cup balsamic vinegar
2 tbs. soy sauce

Wrap the fillets in buttered sheets of aluminum foil. Season with wine, lemon and pepper. Bake in a 450° oven for 5 minutes.

Place the tomatoes in boiling water for 1 minute. Remove from water. Peel and dice them. Mix the other sauce ingredients and pour over tomatoes.

You can make this sauce up to an hour ahead of time and let it stand at room temperature. Spoon the sauce over the fish. *Serves 4.*

Once in a hotel dining room I said, rather too loudly, "I loathe prunes." "So do I," came an unexpected 6-year-old voice from another table. Sympathy was instantaneous. We both knew that prunes are far too nasty to be funny.
C. S. LEWIS, from *Other Worlds: Essays and Stories*

A COIN OF THE REALM

When they reached Capernaum, the collectors of the temple tax came to Peter and said, "Does your teacher not pay the temple tax?" He said, "Yes, he does." And when he came home, Jesus spoke of it first, asking, "What do you think, Simon? From whom do kings of the earth take toll or tribute? From their children or from others?" When Peter said, "From others," Jesus said to him, "Then the children are free. However, so that we do not give offense to them, go to the sea and cast a hook; take the first fish that comes up and when you open its mouth, you will find a coin; take that and give it to them for you and me."
—Matt. 17:24-27

Jesus paid the temple tax miraculously to remind Peter that Jesus was the Son of God, not a subject. The coin in the fish's mouth is the means by which Jesus makes his point. But the coin is also a surprising gift that pays Jesus' and Peter's taxes.

Jesus had the sort of faith in providence that moves mountains and causes fish to suck up coins from the bottom of the sea. For the most part, we can't foretell the specifics of God's providence—but we, nevertheless, place ourselves in God's hands. As Peter says at another time when Jesus asks the twelve whether they wish to leave him, "To whom can we go? You have the words of eternal life." (John 6:68).

Jesus always provides with a flourish, and you can, too, with this easy-to-make recipe.

Imitation Crab Spinach Salad

1 pkg. imitation crab, flaked
1 lb. fresh spinach, cleaned,
  torn, and stems
  removed
1 lb. fresh mushrooms,
  sliced
balsamic vinegar to taste
parmesan cheese (optional)

Toss all ingredients together. Top with parmesan cheese if desired. *Serves 4.*

Whoever really has considered the lilies of the field or the birds of the air and pondered the improbability of their existence in this warm world within the cold and empty stellar distances will hardly balk at the turning of water into wine—which was, after all, a very small miracle. We forget the greater and still continuing miracle by which water (with soil and sunlight) is turned into grapes.

Wendall Berry, from *Sex, Economy, Freedom & Community*

INFANTS IN CHRIST

I could not talk to you as spiritual people, but as fleshly people, as infants in Christ. I fed you with milk, not solid food, for you were not ready for solid food. Even now you are still not ready, for you are still of the flesh. For as long as there is jealousy and quarreling among you, are you not of the flesh, and behaving according to human inclinations?—I Cor. 3:1-3

One time when I was preparing dinner at a local shelter for women and children, we'd gotten a donation of beef and gravy from a caterer— good meat but not enough to go around. So I boiled noodles to stretch it. One of the guests, Sandy, came out to the kitchen and looked in the pots. "McGivern," she said, "this is great. Your making a fantastic dinner. I didn't know you could make such a terrific meal."

That little dig at my culinary skill got under my skin. So I said, "It's almost ready. All I have to do is add the beets. They came in with the donations, and no one will eat them."

"Beets!" It was a cry of horror. "Just wait. Please, don't put them in yet. Promise?"

I promised. Sandy went through the house getting everyone to sign a petition against the beets. For the next 30 minutes, a steady stream of house guests, visitors and staff pleaded with me not to put beets in the stew. I didn't. Sandy got congratulations all around.

I know that beets sometimes make other foods look funny and that attractive meals are important for family and community life. We are all infants in Christ, and we need comfort food. In fact, good food helps us overcome jealousy and quarreling. Sometimes, even beets can be comfort food.

Raspberry Borscht

2 lbs. beets
pinch of salt
1 lb. raspberries
¼ cup red onion, minced
½ cup lemon juice
3 tbs. balsamic vinegar
¼ cup sugar
nonfat sour cream

Scrub the beets, place them in a soup pot and cover with water. Add salt. Simmer until tender, 30 to 45 minutes depending on their size.

Drain, reserving the liquid, and allow the beets to cool at room temperature. Peel and quarter.

Combine beets, raspberries, red onion and 2 cups of reserved liquid. Puree them in a blender and then strain to remove raspberry seeds. Stir in the lemon juice, vinegar and 3 tbs. sugar. Add more sugar if desired. Chill. Serve in chilled bowls with 1 tsp. of sour cream. *Serves 4.*

The time of business does not with me differ from the time of prayer, and in the noise and clatter of my kitchen, while several persons are calling for different things, I possess God in as great tranquility as if I were upon my knees at the blessed sacrament.

Brother Lawrence

BOUNTY

The point is this: that one who sows sparingly will also reap sparingly, and the one who sows bountifully will also reap bountifully. Each of you must give as you have made up your mind, not reluctantly or under compulsion, for God loves a cheerful giver. And God is able to provide you with every blessing in abundance, so that by always having enough of everything you may share abundantly in every good work.—II Cor. 9:6-8

What I've noticed is that as our genuine difficulties decrease, we replace them with problems of our own making, such as road rage, judgments of our neighbors, and fury at the government. It's enough to make one think the sun will never shine and the flowers will never bloom.

Saint Paul reminds us that the Lord loves a cheerful giver. We have so much to fill us with cheer. Whatever the day's difficulties, take them in stride and count God's blessings that surround you. One sunset in a lifetime would have been generous; we've been given so much more. So smile. This spring, cultivate a light heart.

Italian Bean Salad

1 lb. fresh green beans
1 large red potato
1 large tomato, cut into 8
wedges and then halved
¼ medium red onion, diced
1 tablespoon basil, finely
chopped
olive oil to taste
balsamic vinegar to taste

Wash the green beans, snap off and discard ends, place in saucepan. Barely cover beans with water. Bring to a boil and then immediately remove from heat and drain.

Scrub potato, place in a sauce pan, cover with water, bring to boil and boil 10 to 15 minutes, until potato is tender when pierced with a fork. Remove from heat, drain, peel and slice evenly.

Toss the ingredients and serve at room temperature. *Serves 4.*

Happy Home Recipe: 4 cups of love, 2 cups of loyalty, 3 cups of forgiveness, 1 cup of friendship, 5 spoons of hope, 2 spoons of tenderness, 4 quarts of faith, 1 barrel of laughter. Take love and loyalty, mix thoroughly with faith. Blend it with tenderness, kindness and understanding. Add friendship and hope, sprinkle abundantly with laughter. Bake it with sunshine.
Serve daily with generous helpings.

AUTHOR UNKNOWN

WITNESS GOD'S CREATION

Friends, why are you doing this [offering animal sacrifice to Paul]? We are mortals just like you, and we bring you good news, that you should turn from these worthless things to the living God who made the heaven and the earth and the sea and all that is in them. In the past generations he allowed all the nations to follow their own ways; yet he has not left himself without a witness in doing good—giving you rains from heaven and fruitful seasons, and filling you with food and your hearts with joy.—Acts 14:15-17

It's so easy to get caught up in worthless things. We are forever trying to meet our spiritual need—our need for joy—with material goods, such as cars, clothes and furniture. We engage in materialistic activities—shopping, decorating, frivolous movies and computer games—all to evade the living God.

Spring is God's witness. The brilliant chartreuse of new life shimmers through the young leaves and the shoots of new grass. Buds swell; fruit trees blossom; crocuses and tulips peep up; days lengthen; the light grows warmer. If we're stuck in an office all day, it's all the more important that we don't spend the weekend in malls or watching television. Spring is participatory. Meeting spring, we meet God.

If you have no garden or your obligations are heavy, bring spring inside by sprouting beans for salad or egg foo yung.

Bean Sprouts

1 qt. glass jar
a square piece of nylon
(cut from stockings)
seeds for sprouting (mung
bean, alfaïfa, arugula,
watercress or wheat)

Rinse 2 tbs. of sprout seeds twice and place them in a jar. Stretch the nylon over the mouth of the jar and fasten it with a rubber band. Place the jar on its side on a window sill. Rinse the sprouts once a day. In five days the sprouts will be ready to eat.

Egg Foo Yung

2 tbs. peanut oil
½ cup onions, chopped
1 stalk celery, chopped
1 green pepper, chopped
1 cup cooked pork, diced
(or tofu or chicken)
1 jar bean sprouts
(from above)
½ lb. mushrooms, chopped
(optional)
1 can water chestnuts,
chopped (optional)
1 can bamboo shoots
(optional)
¼ tsp. salt
8 eggs, beaten

Sauce
1 cup chicken or
vegetable broth
pepper
2 tsp. tamari or soy sauce
4 tsp. cornstarch

In a large skillet or wok, sauté the fresh vegetables, meat and tofu in peanut oil. Drain the canned vegetables, add them to the skillet and heat. Pour the mixture into a bowl. Add eggs to the mixture. Put half-cupfuls of the mixture onto the hot skillet or wok and fry on both sides. Add more peanut oil to skillet if necessary.

Make a paste by mixing the cornstarch with a little cool broth in a cup. In a saucepan bring the rest of the broth, pepper and tamari sauce to a boil. Add the cornstarch paste. Cook for a minute or so until thick. *Serves 4.*

Summer: Ordinary Time

COME TO THE BANQUET

On one occasion when Jesus was going to the house of a leader of the Pharisees to eat a meal on the Sabbath, they were watching him closely.—Luke 14:1

Jesus' teaching at this banquet is a feast in itself. First, on the way to dinner, Jesus healed a man with dropsy and asked the Pharisees whether it was lawful to do so on the Sabbath. Once he arrived at the host's house, he chided the guests for jockeying to sit at the head of the table. Then he urged them to invite guests too poor to repay the invitation, so that repayment would come at the "resurrection of the righteous" (Luke 14:14).

One of the guests, says Luke, on hearing this, said to Jesus, "Blessed is anyone who will eat bread in the kingdom of God!" (Luke 14:15). Jesus responded by telling the story of the person who gave a great dinner. The invitees were too busy surveying property, buying cows and celebrating honeymoons to attend. The story ends with the host saying, "None of those who were invited will taste my dinner" (Luke 14:24). Being with Jesus at this banquet must have given most of the diners indigestion.

Jesus attends or tells stories of a dozen different dinner parties, banquets and Passover meals in the gospels. Half are etiquette-for-the-kingdom instruction and half testimonials about the life of God. Underlying all Jesus' teachings at these meals is the sense of shared plenty—plenty of food, plenty of guests, plenty of ideas. Jesus uses these moments of festive community to tutor the guests in the meaning of union with God and communion with one another.

Summer, with its abundance of food, fine weather and parties, is a good time to reflect on Jesus' banquet circuit. The recipes themselves make up a menu for a summer banquet.

BITE INTO LIFE

As Jesus was walking along, he saw a man called Matthew sitting at the tax booth; and he said to him, "Follow me." And he got up and followed him.

And as he sat at dinner in the house, many tax collectors and sinners came and were sitting with him and his disciples. When the Pharisees saw this, they said to his disciples, "Why does your teacher eat with tax collectors and sinners?" But when he heard this, he said, "Those who are well have no need of a physician, but those who are sick. Go and learn what this means, 'I desire mercy, not sacrifice.' For I have come to call not the righteous but sinners."
—Matt. 9:9-13

The Pharisees are right that our companions form our characters. Often we're lazy and choose to socialize with those of like mind who offer us little or no challenge. Apparently the Pharisees were lazy, too, and never reached out from their closed circle. The invitation Matthew received from Jesus changed his life, and Jesus wants us to know how important it is to have friends whose minds expand our ideas.

The Pharisees couldn't think big. Nor could they recognize the largeness of Jesus' mind, much less admit that they, too, were sinners. So they missed not only the chance to meet interesting people but the point of Jesus' teaching: that the merciful God desires mercy from us. For all of us who—like the Pharisees—strive to be good, make sacrifices and cast judgment on those we deem morally wrong, that's a teaching with a bite to it.

The roasted garlic below is an interesting hors d'oeuvre with a bite to it. Invite someone to share it with you who stretches your mind and your mercy.

Roasted Garlic and Brie

garlic, unpeeled whole heads, one per guest
olive oil (optional)
crackers or bread
wedge of brie cheese, room temperature

Place the unpeeled head of garlic in the microwave on high for 30 seconds or until the garlic is soft (or coat with olive oil and roast in the oven for 40 minutes at 225°).

Serve with crackers or bread and brie. Let the guests squeeze their own garlic cloves from the skin.

A note about cooking garlic. As a general rule, the longer you cook it, the milder it tastes. But don't let it burn or it will taste bitter.

Father of all, make the roof of my house wide enough for all opinions,
oil the door of my house so it opens easily to friend and stranger,
and set such a table in my house that my whole family may
speak kindly and freely around it.

HAWAIIAN PRAYER,
from *The Complete Book of Common Prayer*

SWEET HOT TIMES

Then they said to him, "John's disciples, like the disciples of the Pharisees, frequently fast and pray, but your disciples eat and drink." Jesus said to them, "You cannot make wedding guests fast while the bridegroom is with them, can you? The days will come when the bridegroom will be taken away from them, and then they will fast in those days."—Luke 5:33-35

The Pharisees were religious authorities, and they demanded rigorous practice of the law. Obedience to the law is not bad, of course, but they never seemed to give anyone a break. They probably didn't enjoy life, and they certainly didn't enjoy Jesus. They didn't ask whether he prayed and fasted regularly; instead, they seemed to resent his pleasures. I suspect they didn't permit themselves much pleasure either—they had soured on life.

Life can be sweet. Taste it. Taste the abundance of summer fun. Summer is like an annual honeymoon: enjoy your spouse, your friends, your neighbors. Take pleasure in the garden and the local farmers' market. Take time to play. Treat your family to celebrations for no reason in particular. Remember that the Bridegroom is always with us.

Mango Salsa and Chips

1 ripe mango
3 Roma tomatoes
1 red onion (medium)
1 red bell pepper (medium)
1 jalapeño pepper (or 6 oz.
    jar, juice discarded)
1 small bunch cilantro
low or nonfat tortilla chips

Dice all the produce into small, same-size pieces and mix together. Refrigerate for at least two hours. Serve with tortilla chips.

For everything there is a season, and a time for every
matter under heaven:
a time to be born, and a time to die;
a time to plant, and a time to pluck up
what is planted;
a time to kill, and a time to heal;
a time to break down, and a time to
build up;
a time to weep, and a time to laugh;
a time to mourn, and a time to dance;
a time to throw away stones, and a time
to gather stones together.

Ecclesiastes 3:1-5

WISDOM WINS THE DAY

"For John came neither eating nor drinking, and they say, 'He has a demon'; the Son of Man came eating and drinking, and they say, 'Look, a glutton and a drunkard, a friend of tax collectors and sinners!' Yet wisdom is vindicated by her deeds."—Matt. 11:18-19

Criticism cuts more keenly for those of us who want to be number one, making everything into contests we can win. Worse, in mainstream American culture, winning is more satisfying if losers suffer. Even when we know that winning isn't the point, we feel worse when we lose than we feel good about winning.

We've become an angry culture, eager to tell one another off and glorify ourselves. But why should we be so mean-spirited when we've been given so much?

Acting out of God's wisdom places us in the path of criticism, but winning and losing by society's standards will become meaningless. Wait and see. We can't make final evaluations until we've lived our lives, or at least finished a chapter of our living. Then we can identify and reflect on the pattern of our behavior and see how God's wisdom has shaped our lives. Have we influenced others for good and let them influence us? Have we been available to others who need us? Have we admitted mistakes and tried to make amends? If we have, we are vindicated, no matter how strong the criticism was in passing.

The lush fullness of summer is a good time to examine our own recent past, forgive ourselves for our failures and omissions, make a firm purpose of amendment, and close our mouths about the failings of others.

MELITZANOSALATA (EGGPLANT SALAD)

1 large eggplant
3 cloves garlic
1 cup plain yogurt
$^{1}/_{3}$ cup olive oil
3 tbs. balsamic vinegar
bread or crackers

Wash the eggplant, cut off the ends, make a slit lengthwise and microwave 5 to 6 minutes (or slice and grill over a hot fire for 2 minutes, or oven bake at 350° for 30 minutes) until soft and tender. Chop in blender (do not remove skin) with garlic and other ingredients for 30 seconds or until all ingredients are mixed but not pureed. Serve with bread or crackers.

See note on eggplant on p. 23.

Why is there war? Why is there hunger? Why is there pain? Perhaps it's an incentive for struggling human beings to reach out to one another, to help one another, to love one another, to be blessed and strengthened and humanized in the process.

THEA BOWMAN, from *Shooting Star*

A DOSE OF VINEGAR

Now the woman was a Gentile, of Syrophoenician origin. She begged him to cast the demon out of her daughter. He said to her, "Let the children be fed first, for it is not fair to take the children's food and throw it to the dogs." But she answered him, "Sir, even the dogs under the table eat the children's crumbs." Then he said to her, "For saying that, you may go—the demon has left your daughter." So she went home, found the child lying on the bed, and the demon gone.—Mark 7:26-30

Imagine the implications of this story—we have the power to persuade Jesus to change his mind! He has a plan, but he will set it aside for our sakes if we ask in good faith. I never used to like this story. Jesus' discrimination against the Gentiles challenged my childish sense of a sweet Jesus. Then, a while back, on the day the annual assembly of my religious community was to vote on establishing a retirement fund for ourselves, we read this passage from scripture. In response to God's word, the community established a hunger fund as well as the retirement fund.

The hunger fund is crumbs from my community's table. It is a salutary dose of vinegar to remind us of a host of contradictions: we must meet the needs of our oldest sisters who have spent their lives for the poor; we must continue to work with and for the poor; we must be responsible stewards, caring for our resources; we must feed the hungry; we can never meet all the needs; we must do what we can.

Many scholars believe that Jesus worked out the elements of his ministry ingredient by ingredient. And this particular ingredient, his treatment of a non-Jewish supplicant, tastes to me like a dose of vinegar. Whole books are written about how vinegar cures colds, arthritis and digestive disorders. Maybe it does. This story in Jesus' life cures me of my desire to fix everything myself, helps me recognize my own limitations, and encourages me to ask God and others for what I need.

Tuna Aspic

1 6-oz. can tuna
1 pkg. unflavored (or lemon)
    gelatin
¼ cup mayonnaise
½ cup celery, chopped fine
½ cup carrots, diced
½ cup cucumber, chopped
2 tsp. pimento, chopped
1½ tsp. balsamic vinegar

GARNISH
pimento
green pepper rings
cucumbers, sliced
mayonnaise

Flake the tuna. Dissolve the gelatin according to package instructions. Add the other ingredients, stirring carefully. Pour into a mold and refrigerate until set.

Garnish with pimento, green pepper rings, sliced cucumbers and mayonnaise before serving. *Serves 6.*

Take care of the crumbs. They are also food. Do not let them fall.
Gather them. Cherish them.

GUNILLA NORRIS, from *Becoming Bread*

MORE VINEGAR

Once more Jesus spoke to them in parables, saying, "The kingdom of God may be compared to a king who gave a wedding banquet for his son. He sent his slaves to call those who had been invited to the wedding banquet, but they would not come. Again he sent other slaves, saying, 'Tell those who have been invited: Look, I have prepared my dinner, my oxen and my fat calves have been slaughtered, and everything is ready; come to the wedding banquet.' But they made light of it and went away, one to his farm, another to his business, while the rest seized his slaves, mistreated them, and killed them. The king was enraged. He sent his troops, destroyed those murderers, and burned their city. Then he said to his slaves, 'The wedding is ready, but those invited were not worthy. Go therefore into the main streets, and invite everyone you find to the wedding banquet.' Those slaves went out into the streets and gathered all whom they found, both good and bad; so the wedding hall was filled with guests.

"But when the king came in to see the guests, he noticed a man there who was not wearing a wedding robe, and he said to him, 'Friend, how did you get in here without a wedding robe?' And he was speechless. Then the king said to the attendants, 'Bind him hand and foot, and throw him into the outer darkness where there will be weeping and gnashing of teeth.' For many are called, but few are chosen."—Matt. 22:1-14

Here's more vinegar. The king has definitely soured on his originally invited guests. The banquet God has set in front of us is a feast of love. He calls us to love one another. But God is a demanding lover.

Vinegar has its paradoxes. It's a sour wine that preserves meats and vegetables, counters the sugar in sweet dishes, and flavors salads. I like vinegar, but I don't understand why it tastes so good. How can I understand or explain the mysteries of God's demanding love? I can't, but I find small kitchen mysteries to remind me that saying yes to God isn't always a sweet experience, but in the long run it satisfies.

SAUTÉED SPINACH WITH BALSAMIC SYRUP

**1 lb fresh spinach, cleaned
  and stems removed**
2 tsp. olive oil
1 clove garlic, minced

SYRUP
½ cup balsamic vinegar
½ cup brown sugar

Sauté the garlic in oil on medium heat. Add the spinach. Toss in a pan while cooking until slightly darkened. Place in a serving bowl.

Combine the vinegar and sugar in a sauce pan over medium heat. Cook about 5 minutes, until thick. Drip mixture over the sautéed spinach. *Serves 4.*

Strange to see how a good dinner and feasting reconciles everybody.
SAMUEL PEPYS

MIND YOUR MANNERS

"Whatever house you enter, first say, 'Peace to this house!' and if anyone is there who shares in peace, your peace will rest on that person; but if not, it will return to you. Remain in the same house, eating and drinking whatever they provide, for the laborer deserves to be paid. Do not move from house to house. Whenever you enter a town and its people welcome you, eat what is set before you; cure the sick who are there, and say to them, 'The kingdom of God has come near to you.' But whenever you enter a town and they do not welcome you, go out into its streets and say, 'Even the dust of your town that clings to our feet, we wipe off in protest against you.'"—Luke 10:5-11

Many of the disciples were unsophisticated. They needed this brief lecture in etiquette from Jesus so they wouldn't say "yuck!" at what their hosts served. We, too, need an occasional lesson in manners—not so much about eating what we are served (although that's a valuable lesson) but about the value of diversity.

Differences make most people uncomfortable, and many of us live our lives in closely controlled, homogeneous communities. We don't meet many people who are very different from us, and when we do, our natural reaction is to recoil rather than embrace. But Jesus tells us to be at peace with diversity, to sit with it and accept it and—just as important—not to fear the rejection of those who see *us* as different.

The recipe that follows is a Greek dish that Jesus' disciples may have encountered in their travels. It offers a combination of sweet and sour ingredients that may surprise some American palates. It is delicious and reminds us to incorporate the wisdom and cultural gifts of others into our lives.

Watermelon with Olives and Feta Cheese

2 tbs. olive oil (optional)
1¼ lb. watermelon, seeded
   and diced (about ⅓
   large watermelon)
⅓ lb. feta cheese
⅓ lb. kalimata olives
2 tbs. fresh basil
pepper to taste

Mix the ingredients and serve chilled.
Serves 8.

The nurturing of the body becomes a metaphor of the mutual nourishing of lives. Every time we hold hands and say a blessing before a meal, every time we lift a glass and say fine words to one another, every time we eat in peace and grace together, we have celebrated the covenants that bind us together.

ROBERT FULGHUM, from *From Beginning to End*

ALL I HAVE IS YOURS

"Get the fatted calf and kill it, and let us eat and celebrate; for this son of mine was dead and is alive again; he was lost and is found." And they began to celebrate! . . .

[The older son said] "Listen! For all these years I have been working like a slave for you, and I have never disobeyed your command; yet you have never given me even a young goat so that I might celebrate with my friends. But when this son of yours came back, who has devoured your property with prostitutes, you killed the fatted calf for him!" Then the father said to him, "Son, you are always with me, and all that is mine is yours. But we had to celebrate and rejoice, because this brother of yours was dead and has come to life; he was lost and has been found."—Luke 15:23-24, 29-31

I feel great joy when the father says to his older son, "You are with me always and all that I have is yours." The son had thought his father was taking him for granted. Now, hearing these words, he felt the force of his father's abiding love.

We usually don't honor one another for hanging in over the years—raising the children, keeping the pantry stocked, getting the vote out, or going to work every day. One of Jesus' many points in this rich and complex story is that we can and should express our love. In fact, that's why we have banquets—to celebrate our joy in one another and share what we have with those we love.

So celebrate the summer and serve lovely food to your guests. Remember to tell them how glad you are to count them as friends.

SCALLOPS WITH LETTUCE SALAD

1 lb. scallops, rinsed
salt
pepper
lemon juice

SALAD
½ lb. spinach
1 bunch French endive
1 bunch leaf lettuce
violet leaves (optional)
lamb's quarters leaves
**   (optional)**
young dandelion leaves
**   (optional)**
day lily flowers (optional)
dandelion flowers (optional)
rose petals (optional)
1 stalk celery, diced
1 bell pepper, diced
½ small onion, diced
bean sprouts
raisins

DRESSING
¼ cup balsamic vinegar

Toss salad ingredients (including optional ones, if desired) in a large bowl.

Add the scallops to 2 cups of boiling water, reduce the heat and simmer for 10 minutes. Drain. (Save the liquid to flavor soup another day.) Add salt, pepper and lemon juice to the scallops and then mix them into the salad. Dress with balsamic vinegar. *Serves 8.*

I never see any home cooking. All I get is fancy stuff.
PRINCE PHILIP, DUKE OF EDINBURGH

CLEAN HEARTS

While he was speaking, a Pharisee invited him to dine with him; so he went in and took his place at the table. The Pharisee was amazed to see that he did not first wash before dinner. Then the Lord said to him, "Now you Pharisees clean the outside of the cup and of the dish, but inside you are full of greed and wickedness. You fools! Did not the one who made the outside make the inside also? So give for alms those things that are within; and see, everything will be clean for you."—Luke 11:37-41

For years, one small effort I made to counter my sins of negligence was to make up a new grace at dinner each evening. But gradually, I came to repeat the same prayer over and over: God grant us the grace to feed the hungry.

There's plenty of food. Our enormous sin of omission in this day and age is that, in our country's great wealth, we throw away our leftovers—food we just blessed. Meanwhile, in developing nations, a third of all children under 5 years of age are stunted because of chronic malnutrition.

We're like the Pharisees. It's difficult to overcome the inertia of our routines. We delay our efforts by making distinctions between the "deserving" and "undeserving" poor. We wash our hands of the slow starvation of the world's children by asking God to feed the hungry but doing little ourselves to bring about a remedy. But we can do something: write a letter to Congress; buy tuna fish or peanut butter for the local food bank; make sandwiches for the soup kitchen that feeds the hungry in town; read some economic analysis; support a farming initiative in a poor nation.

Praying in thanksgiving for our food is a reminder that the hungry are visible if we open our eyes and that we can feed them if we open our hands.

Fresh Tomatoes and Roasted Garlic Pasta

1 lb. pasta (any is fine)
6 ripe tomatoes
1 tbs. salt
¾ tsp. freshly ground black pepper
½ cup roasted garlic (see p. 85)
1 cup loosely packed fresh basil leaves, finely chopped or torn
½ to ¾ cup olive oil
½ cup grated parmesan cheese

Add pasta to boiling water. Cook *al dente* (until tender but slightly chewy). Drain.

Cut tomatoes into pieces into a bowl and add salt and pepper. Stir and set aside for about 15 minutes to allow juices to seep out of tomatoes.

Combine tomatoes with roasted garlic, basil and olive oil. Toss with the cooked pasta and then stir in grated cheese. Serve at room temperature. *Serves 4.*

We say grace before our meals—not to make our food holy, but to acknowledge gratefully that it is already holy. We don't gobble our food, play with it, or throw it around, because food is too sacred to be violated. A "food war" I witnessed in a college cafeteria was one of the most painful desecrations of sacred matter that I have ever suffered.

WILLIAM McNAMARA, from *Christian Mysticism*

WINE TO GLADDEN THE HEART

"And no one puts new wine into old wineskins; otherwise the new wine will burst the skins and will be spilled, and the skins will be destroyed. But new wine must be put into fresh wineskins. And no one after drinking old wine desires new wine, but says, 'The old is good.'"—Luke 5:37-38

As any wine drinker knows, old wine *is* good, with age comes a fullness in flavor and texture. After drinking the richness of the old, no one desires the new. But, alas, what Jesus offers is new wine. It has an unfamiliar flavor, it doesn't go down smoothly and comfortably. It can't be poured into favorite decanters used for aged wines. Jesus' wine is often bitter to taste—we must forgive not seven times but seventy-seven times; we must sell all we have; we must die to ourselves. But when we drink from his cup, we share in eternal life. How sweet it is.

A glass of white wine would go well with the shrimp dish that follows.

Shrimp with Wild Rice

1 cup wild rice
1 cup long-grain rice
½ cup green pepper, diced
½ cup celery, chopped
½ cup scallions, chopped
¼ cup parsley, chopped
1 lb. boiled shrimp, deveined
    and shelled

Dressing
½ cup balsamic vinegar
1 cup olive oil
½ tsp. dry mustard
salt and pepper to taste

Place shrimp in a pot of boiling water and boil about 2 minutes or until shrimp is pink. Drain.

Bring 6 cups of water to a boil. Add the wild rice and cook over moderate heat, covered, for 15 minutes. Add the long grain rice, stir, turn the heat to simmer, cover and cook for 20 minutes.

Remove the rice from the heat and let it stand covered for at least 10 minutes. Drain the rice if necessary. Mix with vegetables and dressing.

Serve on a platter at room temperature with the shrimp heaped in the center of the rice. *Serves 6.*

Eat your bread with enjoyment, and drink your wine with a merry heart.
Ecclesiastes 9:7

DRINK TO LOVE

I have come into my garden, my sister, my bride;
I gather my myrrh with my spice;
I eat my honeycomb with my honey,
I drink my wine with my milk.
Eat, friends, drink, and be drunk with love.—Song of Sol. 5:1

Yes, let's be drunk with love. Love intoxicates us beyond any wine. It is poison to selfishness and worldly ways. When we are truly in love, nothing can reduce the glow—neither sickness nor health; good times nor bad. On the contrary, it's the power of love that enables us to walk through fire and ice and come out of the experience more deeply in love. Passion is a great gift. Honor it.

Lovers, enjoy this delectable berry treat.

BERRIES AND CREAMY YOGURT CHEESE

1 qt. yogurt
1 tsp. vanilla
2 tbs. powdered sugar
1 pint berries

Turn yogurt into creamy yogurt cheese by lining a strainer with cheesecloth or a coffee filter and setting it over a bowl. Place yogurt in the strainer, cover and refrigerate for 4 hours. About half the liquid will drain off. The remaining yogurt cheese can be used in place of cream cheese, sour cream or whipped cream.

Mix the yogurt cheese, vanilla and sugar. Spoon on top of berries. *Serves 4.*

Agape does not begin by discriminating between worthy and unworthy people, or any qualities people possess. It begins by loving others for their sakes.

DR. MARTIN LUTHER KING, from *Stride Toward Freedom*

FRUITFUL ENDEAVORS

"You will know them by their fruits. Are grapes gathered from thorns, or figs from thistles?"—Matt. 7:16

How practical and comforting are these lines of scripture, because they give us a sure measure of our lives. When we ask ourselves whether we are doing God's will, the answer is in the fruits we bear— the work we do, who we count as our friends, how much we share with others and the harmony in our lives.

Each day we are given the opportunity to cooperate in God's creation. We are free to bear figs or thistles, flourish or wither, take root or drift. Which choices will bear fruit? Which will leave us barren?

God doesn't care whether we work or stay home to raise the children, become a nun or a rock star, go to endless political meetings or bake bread from our own starter, as long as we love one another. God loves us for ourselves, not for our choices. But our love for God and others is reflected in those choices. The varieties of human fruitfulness bear witness to God's infinite variety.

LABOR PAINS

Then Jesus went about all the cities and villages, teaching in their synagogues, and proclaiming the good news of the kingdom, and curing every disease and every sickness. When he saw the crowds, he had compassion for them, because they were harassed and helpless, like sheep without a shepherd. Then he said to his disciples, "The harvest is plentiful, but the laborers are few; therefore ask the Lord of the harvest to send out laborers into his harvest."—Matt. 9:35-38

During our lives we will find ourselves as both sheep without a shepherd and as the shepherds themselves; we will be the harvest and the harvesters. Each role is daunting—to both follow Jesus and protect his flock; to be the seed that becomes the mustard tree and to plant and tend that tree. Jesus, too, experienced the pain of life's circumstances: weeping over Jerusalem, suffering the agony in the garden and, here, knowing that he alone could not accomplish his Father's work.

When our own or our neighbors' needs overwhelm us, our comfort is that we are not expected to labor alone. Jesus needs us, and we need his entire Mystical Body—all the saints of heaven and earth. It is our joy to count on one another, confident that together we can feed the hungry, drive the money changers from the temple and build the realm of God.

Gather the strength to labor for the kingdom in the way all good laborers do: by beginning each day with a healthy, hearty breakfast.

GRANOLA

1½ cups rolled oats
1 cup unsweetened coconut,
    shredded
½ cup nuts, chopped
½ cup sesame seeds
½ cup sunflower seeds,
    shelled
½ cup unsweetened wheat
    germ
½ cup honey
¼ cup vegetable oil
½ cup dried fruit
½ cup raisins or pitted dates

Combine the first six ingredients in a large bowl. Separately combine the honey and oil and stir into the oats mixture. Spread onto a 13-by-9-inch pan. Bake at 300°, stirring occasionally, for 45 to 50 minutes or until light brown.

Stir in the dried fruit and raisins. Cool, stirring occasionally to prevent lumping. Store in tightly covered jars or plastic bags. *Makes 6½ cups.*

Cultivators of the earth are the most valuable citizens. They are the most vigorous, the most independent, the most virtuous, and they are tied to their country and wedded to it's liberty and interests by the most lasting bands.

THOMAS JEFFERSON, from *The Papers of Thomas Jefferson*

HONOR THE SAINTS

"Do you not say, 'Four months more, then comes the harvest? But I tell you, look around you, and see how the fields are ripe for harvesting. The reaper is already receiving wages and is gathering fruit for eternal life, so that sower and reaper may rejoice together. For here the saying holds true, 'One sows and another reaps.' I sent you to reap that for which you did not labor. Others have labored, and you have entered into their labor."—John 4:35-38

We don't have to do all the work ourselves. Indeed, our part is quite small. Autumn is a good season to look at all the lives lived before us and marvel at their accomplishments. Jesus asks us to enter into salvation history, joining the saints by continuing their efforts to heal the sick, establish peace, and bring good news to the poor. Our own families were nurtured by our mothers and fathers, grandparents and unknown great-grandparents, to name a few of the saints who have gone before us. We stand on the shoulders of the great men and women of history.

Whose stories do you preserve in your family? Children love hearing stories about their parents' childhoods, stories about grandparents and aunts and uncles. Try making a list of 25 men and women who contributed significantly to human development, including your own. Make it a diverse list, familiar and famous, living and dead, from all the continents, male and female, young and old. Then tell your children about these great men and women—our human heritage.

Preserving memories puts me in mind of preserving food. This recipe for preserved ginger will keep in the refrigerator for several months.

PUREED, PRESERVED GINGER

1 lb. ginger root
1 cup sugar
1 cup water
red food coloring
1 oz. vodka

Peel and thinly slice the ginger root. Boil it on the stove with the sugar and water until the ginger is tender. Puree the mixture in a blender. Add red food coloring and an ounce of vodka as a preservative. Use it to flavor carrots, beets, salad dressing, tuna fish, egg salad, potato salad, rice and sweet soups.

GINGER CARROTS

5 carrots, peeled
1 tsp. raw sugar
2 tsp. pureed ginger (from above)

Shred the carrots in a salad shooter. Add the sugar and ginger. Cover and microwave on high for 2 minutes (or put them in a saucepan, add ¼ cup water and bring to a boil; lower the heat and cook for 1 to 2 minutes). Stir and test for doneness. Use as a hot vegetable or chilled in salad. *Serves 4.*

My Italian relatives . . . always wanted to sit in the kitchen. They even built houses without dining rooms. Big kitchens were all they wanted. They lived their whole lives in those kitchens, around the stove, eating, talking, playing cards, reading newspapers, drinking coffee. When they weren't around the stove, they were in church, in God's home . . .

JO ANN PASSARIELLO DECK, from *Where the Heart Is*

EXPERIENCE OF EVIL

He put before them another parable: "The kingdom of heaven may be com-
pared to someone who sowed good seed in his field; but while everybody was
asleep, an enemy came and sowed weeds among the wheat, and then went
away. So when the plants came up and bore grain, then the weeds appeared as
well. And the slaves of the householder came and said to him, 'Master, did you
not sow good seed in your field? Where, then, did these weeds come from?' He
answered, 'An enemy has done this.' The slaves said to him, 'Then do you want
us to go and gather them?' But he replied, 'No; for in gathering the weeds you
would uproot the wheat along with them. Let both of them grow together until
the harvest; and at harvest time I will tell the reapers, "Collect the weeds first
and bind them in bundles to be burned, but gather the wheat into my
barn.'"—Matt. 13:24-30

From our own experience we know that there is evil in the world—a lot
of evil. Some of it is natural or at least accidental: disease, earthquakes,
famine, floods. But some is human sin: pride, greed, cruelty, hatred.
This parable describes God's realm on earth where evil stands side by side
with good. The only explanation for the evil is that an enemy of God has
caused it.

We have been commissioned to reserve judgment for God, practice
patience with sinners, and try to change minds and hearts. As God's harvesters
we must bring to a caring world's attention institutional structures that cause
death and suffering—war, manufacture of nuclear weapons, high military
budgets, land mines, capital punishment, maldistribution of food and medicine, the growing gap between rich and poor, and corporate greed and waste.

But, of course, as harvesters we also reap what is good. Squash is one of
the great good foods of the fall harvest. It's low in fat and loaded with nutri-
ents and fiber. What's more, its vivid orange color brightens any table setting.

STUFFED SQUASH WITH ORANGE-GINGER SAUCE

**2 medium-sized winter
   squash, halved and
   prebaked**
2 tbs. butter
1 cup onion, minced
½ lb. tofu, diced (optional)
½ lb. mushrooms, minced
1 large clove garlic, minced
1 stalk celery, minced
½ tsp. salt
black pepper
½ tsp. sage
½ tsp. thyme
2 tbs. lemon juice
¼   cup walnuts, minced
¼   cup sunflower seeds
¼   cup raisins
2 cups bread crumbs
**6 to 8 dried apricots
      (optional)**
**1 cup cheddar cheese, grated
      (if tofu is not used)**

ORANGE-GINGER SAUCE
2 tbs. cornstarch
1 cup orange juice
2 to 3 cloves garlic, minced
**1 tbs. fresh ginger, minced
      (or 1 tbs. preserved
      ginger, p. 109)**
¼   cup light soy sauce

Halve the squash and remove seeds. Place the halves upside down on a greased cookie sheet. Add half a cup of water. Bake at 350° for 40 minutes or until tender (or bake the squash whole in a crock pot with ¼ cup water, on high for 1 hour and then on low for 6 hours; then split it and remove the seeds.)

Melt the butter in a large skillet. Sauté the onion and tofu until the onion is translucent. Add the mushrooms, garlic, celery and seasonings. Sauté about 10 minutes. Mix in the remaining ingredients. Fill the squash. Cover and bake for 20 to 30 minutes at 350°.

In a small saucepan, dissolve the cornstarch in orange juice. Add the garlic, ginger and soy sauce. Heat on low, stirring constantly, until sauce thickens. Top the squash with the sauce. *Serves 4.*

THE FOOLISH FARMER

"A sower went out to sow. And as he sowed, some seeds fell on the path, and the birds came and ate them up. Other seeds fell on rocky ground, where they did not have much soil, and they sprang up quickly since they had no depth of soil. But when the sun rose, they were scorched; and since they had no root, they withered away. Other seeds fell among thorns, and the thorns grew up and choked them. Other seeds fell on good soil and brought forth grain, some a hundredfold, some sixty, some thirty."—Matt. 13:3-9

What competent farmer would sow seed on paths or rocks or in a bed of thorns? Competent farmers avoid surprises. So what we have here is a parable about God, the Foolish Farmer.

God laces the world with invitations and signposts in the most unlikely places because God knows that roses can bloom on rocky ledges.

We, on the other hand, are parsimonious with goodness, fearful that we'll feed the undeserving poor or support a drunkard. We're cautious lest someone take advantage of our generosity and somehow waste our good acts or use our good ideas without giving us credit. Jesus changed all the rules. He made foolish farming a virtue.

The seeds of love, kindness, patience and justice are unlimited. There's no end to our capacity for good works. Whether our seeds will bear fruit depends on factors beyond our control, but if we never plant our seed in hopes of finding better soil, there's no chance of growth, much less surprises.

The following recipe uses eggplant, that vegetable of a thousand surprises. It's complex, but it will bear the fruit of a delicious meal.

Stuffed Eggplant with Roasted Pepper Sauce

**2 large eggplants, sliced
   lengthwise, ⅛-inch**
**½ lb. ricotta cheese, extra
   moisture removed**
¼ cup fresh basil, chopped
2 tsp. garlic, chopped
⅓ cup pistachios, ground
**1½ tbs. sun-dried tomatoes,
   chopped**
**⅓ cup parmesan cheese,
   grated**

Lemon Sauce

3 tbs. butter
3 tbs. flour
2 cups strong chicken broth
½ cup Chablis wine
juice of one lemon
pinch of white pepper

Roasted Pepper Sauce

1 tsp. butter
1 tsp. flour
**6-oz. jar of roasted red
   peppers**
½ cup chicken broth
½ cup lemon sauce (above)
**pinch of crushed red
   pepper flakes**

Soak the eggplant in lightly salted water for 20 minutes to remove the bitterness. Rinse it, brush it with olive oil and grill for 1 minute. Set it aside to cool.

Mix the cheeses, basil, garlic, pistachios, and tomatoes. Place 1 tbs. of mixture on the narrow end of each eggplant slice, then roll. Place the seam-side down on an oiled casserole dish. Bake at 350° for 10 minutes or until tender.

Lemon sauce: Melt butter in a saucepan and add the flour. Over low heat, blend with a wire whisk until smooth, about 2 minutes. Slowly add the remaining ingredients, continuing to stir until smooth. Continue cooking for another 3 minutes. Allow to cool. (Store excess for a week in the refrigerator or frozen for two months.)

Roasted Pepper Sauce: Combine butter and flour in pan. Heat and allow to thicken, stirring constantly. Add remaining ingredients to sauce, stirring over low heat until smooth (about 5 minutes). Pour roasted pepper sauce over the stuffed eggplant. *Serves 8.*

OURS FOR THE TAKING

He also said, "The kingdom of God is as if someone would scatter seed on the ground, and would sleep and rise night and day, and the seed would sprout and grow, he does not know how. The earth produces of itself, first the stalk, then the head, then the full grain in the head. But when the grain is ripe, at once he goes in with his sickle, because the harvest has come."—Mark 4:26-29

Think of a time when you've been awed by the kindness of a stranger, by the goodness of a loved one or by the forgiving nature of a perceived enemy. What you've witnessed is the flourishing of God's realm—just as the sower/harvester in this parable marvels at the burgeoning crops. We know not how it happens, but God's love prevails and ripens and we reap the rewards. Share your harvest with others.

Tomato Seasoning Mix

1½ tsp. dried minced onion
1½ tsp. dried crushed
      parsley leaves
1½ tsp. cornstarch
1 tsp. dried green pepper
      flakes
¾ tsp. salt
⅛ tsp. dried minced garlic
½ tsp. granulated sugar
¼ tsp. ground oregano
¼ tsp. ground basil

Cut a 6-inch square of heavy duty aluminum foil. Combine all the ingredients. Mix well. Pour the mixture onto the foil. Fold it airtight and store in a cool dry place. (Use within 6 months.)

Quick Pasta Sauce

2 8-oz. cans tomato sauce
6 tbs. tomato paste
2⅔ cups tomato juice or
      water
1 pkg. tomato seasoning mix
      (above)

Optional additions:
mushrooms, sliced and
      sautéed
ground beef or turkey,
      browned
fresh seasonings *(note: fresh
      seasonings are not as
      strong as dried)*

Mix all ingredients in skillet. Simmer over medium heat for 30 minutes, stirring occasionally.

FAMINE TACTICS

"Let them gather all the food of those good years that are coming, and lay up grain under the authority of Pharaoh for food in the cities, and let them keep it. That food shall be a reserve for the land against the seven years of famine that are to befall the land of Egypt, so that the land may not perish through the famine."—Gen. 41:35-36

The world has always suffered periodic famine. But in the past we neither knew about the suffering of our farthest neighbors nor did we have the means to deliver food to them. Today we know their suffering and have the capacity to redistribute food, medicine, energy and even clean water to any point in the globe. What we lack is the political will.

We deliver high-tech weaponry around the world: land mines to Korea, missiles to Brazil, fighter planes to Indonesia, antiaircraft guns to northern Africa. We've armed all sides in the Middle East. Why is it so difficult to give people enough food and medicine?

A thousand years before Christ, Egypt had a plan to care for its citizens when famine struck. Through Joseph (a foreigner), God told them to develop that plan; they listened and acted. God tells us every day—through news reports, government agencies, and our own eyes and ears—to share our excess with those who have nothing.

The abundance of the fall harvest is one of the signs of God's love. Trees heavy with green and red apples and roadside stands of bright orange pumpkins color autumn months just as the leaves of maples and sycamores do. They remind us to share what we've been given with the least among us.

There's plenty to go around with this vegetarian lasagna trimmed with autumn red peppers.

Vegetarian Lasagna

1 lb. lasagna noodles
2 tsp. oil
4 cloves garlic, minced
1 onion, chopped
1 stalk celery, chopped
1 lb. mushrooms, sliced
1 lb. fresh, cleaned and
    stemmed, or 2 12-oz.
    pkgs. frozen spinach
summer squash or zucchini,
    sliced (optional)
2 cans (28 oz.) tomato
    pieces
1 pt. low-fat or nonfat
    cottage cheese
2 tsp. oregano
2 tsp. dried basil
1 lb. mozzarella cheese,
    shredded (low-fat)
2 red bell peppers, diced
parmesan cheese (nonfat)

Sauté the garlic, onions and celery in olive oil. Add the oregano and basil and mix with the cottage cheese. Place a layer of uncooked lasagna noodles on the bottom of a greased 8-by-12-inch pan. Spread a coat of cottage cheese on the noodles. Layer fresh or frozen spinach on top of the cottage cheese, then mushrooms and squash if desired, then mozzarella cheese, followed by canned tomato pieces.

Place a second layer of uncooked noodles on top of the tomatoes. Repeat layers of cottage cheese, spinach, mushrooms, squash, mozzarella and tomatoes. Place a third layer of all the ingredients. Top with dry noodles. Pour the liquid from the canned tomatoes into the pan.

Bake covered at 350° for an hour. Remove the cover, top with red bell peppers and parmesan cheese, and cook for 10 minutes or until cheese is brown. *Serves 10.*

EXCESS

Then the priest shall turn these into smoke on the altar as a food offering by fire for a pleasing odor. All fat is the Lord's.—Lev. 3:16

I love the sentence, "All fat is the Lord's." I know that it means all wealth and abundance are from God and belong to God. But those of us struggling to resist middle-age spread can chuckle.

And even as we laugh, we can let ourselves think a little more about the hungry. A friend of mine who heads an urban clinic for poor children told me that it took him years to realize the reason for the large number of kids in his office clutching potato chip bags. Potato chips are low in cost, high in fat and very filling.

Of course, potato chips are a bad buy if you want nourishment. But nourishing foods—such as fresh fruit and vegetables—are more expensive, particularly in urban areas. It costs a little more to take the fat out of cheese or to leave the pulpy fiber in orange juice.

Remember, all fat is the Lord's. Do with your excess what the Lord would have you do—give it to the poor.

Baked Ziti

16 oz. ziti noodles
8 oz. fat-free mozzarella
    cheese
8 oz. fat-free ricotta cheese
2 cups pasta sauce
    (from a jar or see
    pasta sauce recipe
    on p. 115)
2 tbs. parmesan cheese

Add ziti to boiling water. Cook *al dente* (until tender but slightly chewy). Drain.

Mix the cooked noodles with the ricotta cheese and half the tomato sauce and half the mozzarella cheese. Pour the mixture into a lightly greased baking dish. Top with remaining tomato sauce and mozzarella cheese and the parmesan cheese; cover and bake at 350° for 40 minutes or until it bubbles and the cheese is melted. *Serves 6.*

The bread you store up belongs to the hungry; the cloak that lies in your chest belongs to the naked; the gold that you have hidden in the ground belongs to the poor. If everyone would take only according to his or her needs and would leave the surplus to the needy, no one would be rich, no one poor, no one in misery.

SAINT BASIL THE GREAT

LOVE THE STRANGER

For the Lord your God is God of gods and Lord of lords, the great God, mighty and awesome, who is not partial and takes no bribe, who executes justice for the orphan and the widow, and who loves the strangers, providing them food and clothing. You shall also love the stranger, for you were strangers in the land of Egypt.—Deut. 10:17-19

On one Friday after a Thanksgiving dinner, I took stock of the menu: turkey, mashed potatoes, sweet potatoes, dressing, broccoli, cranberry Jell-O, cranberries, pumpkin and mincemeat pies. During the next year, I went looking for some cultural variations. Add a little diversity to your own Thanksgiving celebration. It's a way to show love for the stranger—for we have all been strangers.

CHITTERLINGS AND HOG MAWS

Chitterlings (or chitlins) are the skins of pig intestines. Chitterlings are cheap but take a long time to prepare; before boiling, they must be cleaned and the fat removed. You can buy them frozen (picked and cleaned). The hog maw is the stomach. Chitterlings have a mild taste, but an acrid odor while cooking; the odor is cut by the hog maws (which are eaten too).

5 lbs. chitterlings, picked and cleaned
1 hog maw (about ½ lb.)
2 large onions, peeled
1 tbs. salt

1 bunch mustard greens,
1 tbs. prepared mustard or 1 tsp. dry mustard
1 tbs. pepper or peppercorns
hot sauce and prepared mustard

Put all the ingredients but the hot sauce together in a pot, covered with water and boil for about 3 hours, until the hog maw is dark and the chitterlings are very tender. Drain, discard the onion and greens and serve with hot sauce and mustard. (Cooked chitterlings can also be dipped in a batter and deep-fried.) *Serves 5 to 10 as a side dish.*

TURKEY GUMBO

turkey carcass, well picked
2 onions, sliced
gravy and or turkey drippings
flour (if using drippings)
turkey meat scraps
leftover turkey dressing
1 10-oz. can tomatoes

1 lb. fresh or 1 12-oz. pkg. frozen
   okra
2 bay leaves
1 tsp. curry powder
2 tsp. gumbo filé
cooked rice (see p. 135)

In a large soup pot, cover the turkey carcass with water and bring to a low boil. Simmer for 3 to 4 hours, adding water if necessary. Allow to cool and remove all the bones and bits of gristle. This is most easily done by straining it through a colander and then returning the bits of meat to the soup stock.

In a separate pan, sauté the onions in gravy or turkey drippings. If you are using drippings, add 1 tbs. flour for every 2 tbs. drippings and stir to thicken. Add the onions, gravy and remaining ingredients, except for the rice, to the stock and heat to a low simmer. Allow it to cook without boiling for at least 1 hour, preferably 2 or 3. Serve over cooked rice.

CRANBERRY SOUP

1 lb. fresh or frozen cranberries
2 cups water
2 cups sugar
1 cup burgundy wine
1 tbs. cornstarch

1 stick cinnamon
½ tsp. lemon peel
sour cream garnish
orange or lemon peel garnish

Mix the berries, water and sugar in a pot. Bring to a boil and cook until the berries pop. Pour the broth through a colander to strain out the cranberry skins. This step can be done well in advance of dinner.

Return the cranberry broth to the stove on low heat. Mix the wine and cornstarch together and add slowly to simmering broth. Add the cinnamon stick and lemon peel and stir until the soup thickens. Garnish and serve.

Advent

KNOWING OURSELVES, KNOWING GOD

"I baptize you with water for repentance, but one who is more powerful than I is coming after me; I am not worthy to carry his sandals. He will baptize you with the Holy Spirit and fire. His winnowing fork is in his hand, and he will clear his threshing floor and will gather his wheat into the granary; but the chaff he will burn with unquenchable fire."—Matt. 3:11-12

Advent poses the questions, Who am I? and Who is God? They go together. John the Baptist acknowledged repentant sinners, welcomed them and cleansed them symbolically with water—because he knew he was a sinner himself. He had come to terms with his own powerlessness. It was because he knew and accepted himself that he was able to recognize God in the person of Jesus.

John's harsh images burn brightly and uncompromisingly in contrast with these darkest days of winter, when the damp cold chills our confidence in God. But Jesus has come and has baptized us already. We are cleansed by his baptism of fire, and we live in the Holy Spirit.

This power of Jesus is awesome. John's heightened language describes Jesus as the harvester who burns the chaff as well as stores the grain. The shortening daylight reminds us to open our eyes a little wider when we look inside ourselves. As we learn more about how to repent and love ourselves, we will better recognize as the signs of God's forgiveness the people around us and the warm bread on our tables.

GOD THE COOK

When they had gone ashore, they saw a charcoal fire there, with fish on it, and bread. Jesus said to them, "Bring some of the fish that you have just caught." So Simon Peter went aboard and hauled the net ashore, full of large fish, a hundred fifty-three of them; and though there were so many, the net was not torn. Jesus said to them, "Come and have breakfast." Now none of the disciples dared to ask him, "Who are you?" because they knew it was the Lord. Jesus came and took the bread and gave it to them, and did the same with the fish.—John 21:9-13

In fine restaurants the chef is treated like a god. Here we see a short-order breakfast cook who *is* God. The experience is so unnerving that the fishers (Peter, Thomas, Nathanael, James, John, and two other unnamed disciples) busied themselves counting and sorting fish, not speaking to the resurrected Jesus—though they recognized him.

Even after his resurrection, Jesus remains a servant, the same person who was born in a stable, encouraged children to sit at his knee, and made sure the girl he brought back to life was well fed. Perhaps what made it difficult for the disciples to recognize him was that he wasn't what they had wanted—a great political and military leader. He wasn't even a great chef, just a competent fire builder and griller of fish served with bread.

Oh, to be treated like great chefs ourselves! Ordinary people who cook get very little honor. But as we appreciate our own efforts to get food on the table every day—whether homemade or takeout—we can catch sight of God in ourselves, in the family, friends and strangers we serve, and in the strangers who serve us.

Quiche with Crab

3 tbs. olive oil
½ lb. mushrooms, coarsely chopped
½ cup crackers, finely crushed
2 tbs. olive oil
¾ cup green onions, finely chopped
2 cups Swiss cheese, shredded
1 cup low or nonfat cottage cheese
3 eggs
¼ tsp. ground cayenne pepper
¼ tsp. paprika
1 can (4 oz.) crab meat

In a skillet, heat 3 tbs. olive oil and sauté the mushrooms until limp. Remove them from the heat, stir in the crackers to make a sticky mixture, and turn the mixture into a greased 9-inch pie plate, pressing the dough evenly onto the bottom and sides.

In the same skillet, heat 2 tbs. of olive oil and sauté the onions until transparent. Layer them over the mushroom and cracker crust. Next, layer on the Swiss cheese. In a blender or food processor, mix the cottage cheese, eggs and seasoning. Stir in the crab and pour onto the crust in the pie plate.

Bake at 350° for 20-25 minutes or until a knife stuck into the center comes out clean. *Serves 6.*

I take our plates, spoon eggs on them, we sit and eat. She and I and the kitchen have become extraordinary: we are not simply eating; we are pausing in the march to perform an act together; we are in love; and the meal offered and received is a sacrament which says: I know you will die; I am sharing food with you; it is all I can do, and it is everything.

ANDRE DUBUS, from *Broken Vessels*

WHO IS GOD?

Then the righteous will answer him, "Lord, when was it that we saw you hungry and gave you food, or thirsty and gave you something to drink? And when was it that we saw you a stranger and welcomed you, or naked and gave you clothing? And when was it that we saw you sick or in prison and visited you?" and the king will answer them, "Truly I tell you, just as you did it to one of the least of these who are members of my family, you did it to me."
—Matt. 25:37-40

Here is the hard truth, the one we try to close our eyes to: beggars, addicts, prostitutes, the sick poor, and even death-row inmates are all members of God's family. When we see them and respond with love, we see and respond to God. If we don't see Jesus in the poor, we won't see Jesus at all.

Society is harsh. We punish the least among us. We don't recognize life—much less food, shelter or health care—as a right. We give the poor minimal, low-quality education and put them in prison and on death row in wildly disproportional numbers. We place the poor in a double bind—expecting them to pull themselves up by their boot straps, though we've stolen their boots.

Who are the rich? Most likely anyone reading this book. We call ourselves middle class or working poor, but our children are well nourished and our life expectancy is long. We are wealthy beyond the wildest dreams of most of the human race.

Jesus' words to his disciples here is a call to transformation. Feeding the poor and visiting prisoners will change us. We see God more in ourselves and others when we serve the poor. Our hearts open; we're easier with the fact that our deeds are small; we're surer that it's God who saves; we love the destitute more easily; we know God in them more surely. We are transformed.

I offer below the richest recipe in the book. Sometimes a rich meal reminds us better of our obligations to the poor.

Roast Pork in Milk

2 lbs. pork roast
1 tbs. butter
2 tbs. vegetable oil
1 tsp. salt
fresh ground pepper
2½ cups milk

On the stove, heat the butter and oil in a stovepot pan (with lid) just large enough for the pork. Season the pork, place it fat side down and brown it, then brown the other sides. Slowly add milk to cover the pork and bring it to a boil. Then turn the stove burner to low, cover the pan with the lid askew and simmer for 1½ to 2 hours, until the pork is tender. Add milk as necessary and turn the pork occasionally. The milk will coagulate in clusters, and that's just fine.

Draw some of the fat off the milky liquid into a saucepan. Add 2 to 3 tbs. water and boil away the water to make a sauce. Remove the pork from the pan, spoon the sauce over it and serve. (Reserve the milky liquid to store any leftovers.) *Serves 6.*

I have the audacity to believe that people everywhere can have three meals a day for their bodies, education and culture for their minds, and dignity, equality, and freedom for their spirit.

Dr. Martin Luther King, Jr.

RECOGNIZING POWER

On the third day there was a wedding in Cana of Galilee, and the mother of Jesus was there. Jesus and his disciples had also been invited to the wedding. When the wine gave out, the mother of Jesus said to him, "They have no wine." And Jesus said to her, "Woman, what concern is that to you and to me? My hour has not yet come." His mother said to the servants, "Do whatever he tells you." Now standing there were six stone water jars for the Jewish rites of purification, each holding twenty or thirty gallons. Jesus said to them, "Fill the jars with water." And they filled them up to the brim. He said to them, "Now draw some out, and take it to the chief steward." So they took it. When the steward tasted the water that had become wine, and did not know where it came from (though the servants who had drawn the water knew), the steward called the bridegroom and said to him, "Everyone serves the good wine first, and then the inferior wine after the guests have become drunk. But you have kept the good wine until now." Jesus did this, the first of his signs, in Cana of Galilee, and revealed his glory; and his disciples believed in him.—John 2:1-11

Mary behaves just like a mother. She sees the problem and, utterly confident that her son can fix it, tells the servants to obey him. But how much did she really know about the power of Jesus? Mary's worry for her child when he left her and Joseph to stay at the temple leads us to believe that she must have considered him a normal son. She didn't have any reason to expect miracles from him. Yet she recognized the power of God in him.

Mary pushed her son into revealing his power before he was ready to do it. She recognized his power before he did, whether or not she understood it. She watched and prayed and recognized God. Then she acted on her recognition, calling Jesus to act. We all have power. Mostly it goes unused while we wail about how dreadful things are. Mary is a great model for recognizing God and calling on God's power.

Sweet potatoes are a powerful vegetable, packed with vitamins and minerals. They're an ideal complement to roast pork (see recipe on p. 121).

Sweet Potatoes with Cider Vinaigrette

1½ lbs. sweet potatoes (two large)
2 tbs. olive oil
¼ cup green onions, thinly sliced
2 tbs. cider vinegar

Rub 1 tbs. olive oil on the potatoes and bake at 400° until tender, about an hour. Let potatoes cool a bit, then peel and cut them in 1-inch pieces, put the pieces into a bowl, and sprinkle them with onions. Whisk the remaining oil and vinegar; pour it over the potatoes; toss and serve at room temperature. *Serves 4.*

I pray that, according to the riches of his glory, he may grant that you may be strengthened in your inner being with power through his Spirit and that Christ may dwell in your hearts through faith, as you are being rooted and grounded in love. I pray that you may have the power to comprehend, with all the saints, what is the breadth and length and height and depth, and to know the love of Christ that surpasses knowledge, so that you may be filled with all the fullness of God.

Ephesians 3:16-19

PAY ATTENTION

Six days before the Passover Jesus came to Bethany, the home of Lazarus, whom he had raised from the dead. There they gave a dinner for him. Martha served, and Lazarus was one of those at the table with him. Mary took a pound of costly perfume made of pure nard, anointed Jesus' feet, and wiped them with her hair. The house was filled with the fragrance of the perfume. But Judas Iscariot, one of his disciples (the one who was about to betray him), said, "Why was this perfume not sold for three hundred denarii and the money given to the poor?" (He said this not because he cared about the poor, but because he was a thief; he kept the common purse and used to steal what was put into it.) Jesus said, "Leave her alone. She bought it so that she might keep it for the day of my burial. You always have the poor with you, but you do not always have me."—John 12:1-8

Mary of Bethany is a dramatic figure in scripture. She doesn't do anything half way. She irritates most of the people around her. Once again, as she did earlier in the gospels (Luke 10:38-42), while her sister Martha prepares the meal, Mary kneels at Jesus' feet. Judas challenges her, and John, who is telling the story, warns us of Judas' bad character. But Judas was probably voicing the concern, even alarm, of the other guests. And Jesus isn't reassuring. He talks of his death—a depressing dinner table topic. That's the sort of guest Jesus was—not just unconventional, but downright upsetting.

The meal is the daily practice of community, of life lived in common. Words said at the meal should be honored as important by everyone. That's the ideal. But kids spill milk, spouses have bad days, and guests may be boring or confrontational—all are irritants, like Mary of Bethany. It's easy to miss seeing God in them. Yet family dinners for all their chaos and confusion are where we meet one another. They're important.

Try serving this aromatic stew to put you in mind of Mary of Bethany and her perfume.

ARGENTINIAN STEW

3 tbs. olive oil
2 lbs. stew beef, cut into
    1-inch cubes
4 large tomatoes, coarsely
    chopped
2 onions, coarsely chopped
1 large green bell pepper,
    coarsely chopped
2 large garlic cloves, minced
2 bay leaves
1 tsp. dried oregano,
    crumbled
salt and freshly ground
    pepper
2 cups chicken, beef or
    vegetable broth
1 cup dry white wine
3 large sweet potatoes, cut
    into ½ -inch cubes
2 ears corn, husked and cut
    into 1-inch segments
    (optional)
2 medium zucchini, cut into
    ½ -inch cubes
2 medium pears, cored and
    cut into ½ -inch cubes
2 medium peaches, pitted
    and cut into ½ -inch
    cubes

Heat the oil in a heavy Dutch oven over medium high heat. Add the beef in batches and brown on all sides, about 10 minutes.

Remove from the pan. Add the tomatoes, onion, peppers and garlic to the pan. Reduce the heat to medium and cook until the vegetables are tender, about 10 minutes. Mix in the seasonings; add salt and pepper to taste. Add the stock and wine. Bring to a low boil. Return the beef to pan. Reduce the heat and cover. Simmer for 30 minutes.

Add the potatoes. Recover and simmer for 15 minutes. Add the corn and zucchini and simmer for 10 more minutes. Mix in pears and peaches. Simmer for 5 more minutes. *Serves 8.*

ESSENTIAL TRUTHS

A Samaritan woman came to draw water, and Jesus said to her, "Give me a drink." (His disciples had gone to the city to buy food.) . . . Then the woman left her water jar and went back to the city. She said to the people, "Come and see a man who told me everything I have ever done! He cannot be the Messiah, can he?"—John 4:7-8; 28-29

Jesus is thirsty and he asks a Samaritan woman for water, but at the same time he tells the woman, "Everyone who drinks this water will be thirsty again, but those who drink of the water I will give them will never be thirsty. The water that I will give will become in them a spring of water gushing up to eternal life" (John 4:13-14). When the disciples return with the food they went to get, Jesus tells them that he has "food to eat that you do not know about" (John 4:32). The disciples think that someone else has brought him food, but the woman begins to draw out the deeper meaning of Jesus' words.

Two thousand years later, we still have not tapped the depth of Jesus' meaning. We put food and drink on our table every day. We know they are essential. It's because they are essential that they serve as points of access to God. Eating, we understand the spirit needs food, too. Drinking, we can imagine a fountain that wells up to carry us past death to eternal life.

Setting the table, boiling some pasta and dishing up a meal, we have a chance to contemplate the mystery of Jesus' incarnation. This conundrum of body and soul is the mystical theme of Advent and Christmas. There's no reason why a moment of mystical union with God can't be had while draining the spaghetti for this next meal—just be careful not to burn yourself!

Pasta with Anchovies

½ lb. spaghetti
¼ cup olive oil
2 cloves garlic, minced
1½ lbs. fresh tomatoes
  (4 large or 2 10-oz. can
  whole)
12 green olives
4-6 flat anchovies (may use
  paste)
½ cup fresh parsley,
  chopped
1 tsp. capers, drained
2 tsp. basil, fresh chopped or
  ½ tsp. dried crumbled
½ tsp. dried oregano,
  crumbled
½ tsp. salt
¼ tsp. dried red pepper
  flakes
parmesan cheese

Add spaghetti to boiling water. Cook *al dente* (until tender but slightly chewy). Drain.

Heat the oil; add garlic and sauté for 1 minute; then add remaining ingredients one by one. Continue cooking and stirring until sauce thickens, about 10 minutes. Serve over spaghetti with parmesan cheese. Few will identify the anchovies, the mystery ingredient. *Serves 2.*

The kitchen is a place that sharpens us. It's a place that wakes us up. Our sense of smell becomes keener. We taste with greater subtlety. We see with more clarity and our movements become quick and sure. . . .Cooking requires that we be fully present. This is one of its greatest teachings.

Bettina Vitell, from *A Taste of Heaven and Earth*

THE SPICES OF OUR LIVES

"Woe to you, scribes and Pharisees, hypocrites! For you tithe mint, dill, and cumin, and have neglected the weightier matters of the law: justice and mercy and faith."—Matt. 23:23

What an odd juxtaposition—mint, dill, and cumin up against justice, mercy and faith! The produce of the land, including spices, were once part of the wealth that was tithed for charity. Even today, spices are expensive.

Sometimes we confuse justice with vengeance, as in the case of sentencing a mentally disabled youth to death instead of granting mercy. Or we confuse it with honor by acclaiming a greedy corporate mogul because he or she is rich, instead of inviting him or her to repent. We are also suspicious of mercy, doubting the generosity of God. We don't even give our kids much of a break, but hold mercilessly to rules instead.

In the end, it's our faith that sustains us. Because we are confident in God, we can afford to be just and merciful.

Today, while you chop vegetables for dinner, make up a litany of the people who spice your life and ask God to have mercy on them all. Pray that God will permeate the world with mercy and forgiveness, as the garlic and ginger pervade this next meal.

Rice with Stir-Fried Chicken

Rice
1 cup white rice

Stir-fried Chicken
1 lb. chicken breast, boned,
**   skinned, cut into**
**   ½ -inch cubes**
1 egg white
1 tbs. light soy sauce
1 tsp. sherry
1 tbs. cornstarch
4 cups oil for deep frying
1 tbs. ginger, chopped fine
1 scallion, chopped fine
3 cloves garlic, chopped fine
½ tsp. red pepper flakes

Sauce
1 tsp. sherry
1 tbs. soy sauce
1 tsp. sugar
1 tsp. sesame seed oil
1 tsp. red wine vinegar
1 tsp. cornstarch
¼ tsp. pepper

Bring two cups of water to a rolling boil. Add one cup of plain white rice. Stir and cover. Lower the heat to simmer. Let cook for 20 minutes. Remove from heat. Leave covered until ready to serve. (The secret of perfect rice is low heat and not removing the cover even once while it's cooking.)

Combine the chicken with the egg white, soy sauce, sherry and cornstarch. Mix well. Set aside. Blend the sauce ingredients in a small bowl and set aside. Heat the oil to 350° in a wok or nonstick skillet. Deep fry the chicken about 45 seconds. Remove chicken from oil and drain on a paper towel. (Reserve oil for another time.)

Reheat 1 tbs. of oil in the wok or in a separate skillet. Add the ginger, scallion, garlic and pepper flakes. Stir-fry about 30 seconds (until you can smell it). Add the chicken. Stir-fry 1 more minute. Pour in the sauce mixture. Stir-fry on high heat 10 more seconds. Serve with rice. *Serves 4.*

TAKE A GOOD LOOK

He entered Jericho and was passing through it. A man was there named Zacchaeus; he was a chief tax collector and was rich. He was trying to see who Jesus was, but on account of the crowd he could not, because he was short in stature. So he ran ahead and climbed a sycamore tree to see him, because he was going to pass that way. When Jesus came to the place, he looked up and said to him, "Zacchaeus, hurry and come down, for I must stay at your house today." So he hurried down and was happy to welcome him. All who saw it began to grumble and said, "He has gone to be the guest of one who is a sinner." Zacchaeus stood there and said to the Lord, "Look, half my possessions, Lord, I will give to the poor; and if I have defrauded anyone of anything, I will pay back four times as much." Then Jesus said to him, "Today salvation has come to this house, because he too is a son of Abraham. For the Son of Man came to seek out and to save the lost."—Luke 19:1-10

Zacchaeus was trying to see who Jesus was, but Jesus recognized Zacchaeus first—he saw into his soul. Because of Zacchaeus' willingness to welcome God, he was able to see himself as a sinner and sought to make amends. Zacchaeus promptly embarked on the path of redemption.

Truly welcoming love in our lives always results in a feeling of unworthiness—we can't help but ask, "What did I do to deserve this wonderful blessing?" But sometimes we have to go out of our way to see who God is. Be like Zacchaeus, branch out, take risks, do what you can to get a better glimpse of God. Start with recognizing God in others.

The recipe below is quite elaborate. As you make the filling and wrap it in the leaves, consider everyone who will eat this meal—do what you can to get a better look at the divine life wrapped within them.

Stuffed Grape Leaves

medium-sized stove pot
heatproof plate that fits
    inside pot
medium-sized rock
1 cup cooked rice
    (see p. 135)
½ to 1 lb. lamb, ground
1 tsp. allspice
½ tsp. black pepper
1 tsp. dried mint
1 10-oz. jar brined grape
    leaves
2 lemons
½ cup pine nuts, lightly
    toasted in oven at 150°
    for 30 minutes
water or chicken broth

Garnish
8 oz. nonfat yogurt
1 cucumber, grated
salt and pepper
1 tbs. mint leaves
1 tbs. olive oil

Optional vegetarian recipe:
Replace lamb with
½ cup currants
¼ cup chopped walnuts
and eliminate the pine nuts.

Knead the rice, lamb and dry seasonings to form a dough-like mixture. Remove the grape leaves gently from the jar and rinse well under cold running water. Place a grape leaf on a flat surface, shiny side down. Shape about 1½ tbs. of the meat mixture in a log shape about 2 inches long, and place it on the grape leaf perpendicular to the stem, where the stem joins the leaf; turn the sides of the leaf in and roll from the stem to the outer point. Place the stuffed leaves seam-side down in a medium-sized pot. Repeat until one layer of stuffed leaves covers the bottom of the pot snugly. Squeeze lemon juice generously over the leaves and sprinkle with pine nuts.

Add second and third layers of leaves until the meat stuffing is used up. Place the small plate upside down over the leaves, then put the medium-sized rock gently on the plate. Pour water or broth into the pot just to the level of the saucer. Heat to a very lively simmer and cook about 45 minutes, adding more liquid if needed. Cut one in half to be sure the lamb is well cooked.

Mix the yogurt, grated cucumber, salt, pepper, mint leaves and olive oil in a bowl. Serve as a garnish. *Serves 4.*

Christmas

GOOD THINGS AND GLAD TIDINGS

He has filled the hungry with good things,
and sent the rich away empty.—Luke 1:53

Jesus was born in a stable, lived among the poor and died on a cross. Strangely, many Christians celebrate his birth with an orgy of materialism. The year he started elementary school, one of my nephews asked for simple presents for Christmas. He was delighted with his gifts, but upon returning to school in January, he discovered that the other children had received more elaborate gifts and he asked his parents why. At first, his parents felt terrible—worse, really, than their son. But as their son continued to enjoy the gifts he had received, they relaxed, realizing that they were filling their hungry child with love—not expensive things.

Our society has many things born of our wealth, and they leave us not just empty but filled with the sins of materialism: covetousness, rage or despair at unfair distribution of goods. This simple cookbook, written for busy households, is not a manual for social change, yet our choices in the kitchen do matter, and the truths we discover over our stoves will rise like leaven, flavor us like garlic, scent the house with the odor of sanctity, and bless our lives and the lives of those we love. During Christmas, as you make good food to fill your family and friends, ponder Mary's proclamation of the greatness of God, who fills the hungry with good things.

SCENTED MEMORIES

On entering the house, they saw the child with Mary his mother and they knelt down and paid him homage. Then, opening their treasure chests, they offered him gifts of gold, frankincense, and myrrh.—Matt. 2:11

Frankincense is an incense; myrrh a perfume. Along with gold, they were gifts fit for a king, and they filled the stable's moldering hay and musky animals with a spicy aroma that must have stayed in Mary and Joseph's memory all their lives. The scent of anything like it would carry them back to that stable where Jesus was born.

The scents of the pine trees, turkey, pumpkin pie, hot cider and cinnamon sticks carry many of us back to the Christmases of our youth. These holidays seemed ideal; and we try to recapture them by buying more than we can afford, doing more than we have the energy for, and expecting love and gratitude for our efforts. No wonder we end up exhausted and depressed.

Whether or not the Christmases of our youth were ideal, what matters is our adult choice to give homage to God.

If we can link the perfume of Christmas with the gospel narratives, then the scent of pine trees decorated at Christmas or unadorned in midsummer will remind us that God is with us. That is a memory worth savoring.

Very Low Fat Pumpkin Pie

Pie Crust
12 single squares of graham crackers, crumbled
¼ tsp. cinnamon
⅛ tsp. nutmeg
4 tsp. margarine, melted

Filling
2 envelopes gelatin
1 16-oz. can pumpkin
1⅓ cups nonfat dry milk
1 tsp. pumpkin pie spice
½ cup brown sugar
¼ tsp. rum extract (optional)

Combine the graham cracker crumbs, cinnamon and nutmeg. Add the margarine and mix thoroughly. Spray a 10-inch pie plate with nonstick cooking spray. Press the crust into the plate with the back of a spoon. Bake at 375° 8 to 10 minutes, or until the crust is slightly browned. Let it cool before adding the filling.

Heat 2 cups of water in a large saucepan, then add the gelatin. Stir until dissolved. Add the pumpkin, dry milk, pumpkin pie spice, sugar and rum extract in that order. Cook 10 to 15 minutes over low heat. Stir while simmering. Pour into the pie shell. Refrigerate for at least an hour before serving. *Serves 6 to 8.*

Lift up your heart to God, sometimes even during your meals and when you are in company. The least little remembrance will always be acceptable. You need not cry very loud; God is nearer than we are aware of.

Brother Lawrence

HOW TO MAKE "MERRY"

Then he told them a parable: "The land of a rich man produced abundantly. And he thought to himself, 'What should I do, for I have no place to store my crops?' Then he said, 'I will do this: I will pull down my barns and build larger ones, and there I will store all my grain and my goods. And I will say to my soul, Soul, you have ample goods laid up for many years; relax, eat, drink, be merry.' But God said to him, 'You fool! This very night your life is being demanded of you. And the things you have prepared, whose will they be?' So it is with those who store up treasures for themselves but are not rich toward God."—Luke 12:16-21

At Christmas we are tempted to give way to sentimentality. But an overemotional focus on children blurs Jesus' birth, dirt poor, in a stable. He was born to suffer, die and rise again and to lead us through our own deaths and rebirths. The birth of Christ is indeed cause for celebration. But the celebration should be a heartfelt reminder of God's demands.

One way to encourage this memory is to create traditions. Buying and decorating the tree together as a family gives everyone the opportunity to share their memories and reflections. Keeping secrets, preparing food together, and giving fewer and simpler gifts all enhance the excitement of Christmas without undermining its meaning.

God's gifts to us are extravagant, and Christmas is an extravagant feast. I offer this rich fruitcake recipe as a delicious addition to your Christmas traditions. Making fruitcake provides an opportunity for household members to share in preparation for the feast and experience the preparation itself as an merry moment in the year.

Traditional Fruitcake

2 cups raisins
1 can (16 oz.) cling peaches,
    drained and chopped
1 cup vegetable shortening
1 cup firmly packed brown
    sugar
½ cup cream sherry or
    orange juice
16 oz. mixed candied
    fruits
2 cups chopped walnuts
4 eggs, beaten
2½ cups sifted all purpose
    flour
1 tsp. baking powder
1½ tsp. salt
1 tsp. ground cinnamon
½ tsp. ground cloves
brandy (optional)

Grease and flour two 26-oz. or four 13-oz. coffee cans, or line two muffin tins with cupcake liners.

Combine the raisins, peaches, shortening, brown sugar and sherry in a stove pot. Heat until the shortening is melted and the raisins are plumping. Cool slightly. Add the fruits and nuts, then the eggs. Add the dry ingredients. Mix thoroughly. Fill the pans about half way. Bake at 300° for 2 hours if using coffee cans or 30 minutes if using muffin tins. When ready, the cake will rise slightly, pull away from the edges of the pan and bounce back when pressed.

Pour 1 or 2 tablespoons of brandy over the cooled cakes.

The cakes can be left in coffee tins, covered with plastic lids, and sent as holiday gifts.

We live in a vastly complex society which has been able to provide us with a multitude of material things, and this is good, but people are beginning to suspect that we have paid a high spiritual price for our plenty.

Euell Gibbons, from *Stalking the Wild Asparagus*

FEED MY SHEEP

When they had finished breakfast, Jesus said to Simon Peter, "Simon son of John, do you love me more than these?" He said to him, "Yes, Lord; you know that I love you." Jesus said to him, "Feed my lambs." A second time he said to him, Simon son of John, do you love me?" He said to him, "Yes, Lord; you know that I love you." Jesus said to him, "Tend my sheep." He said to him the third time, "Simon son of John, do you love me?" Peter felt hurt because he said to him the third time, "Do you love me?" And he said to him, "Lord, you know everything; you know that I love you." Jesus said to him, "Feed my sheep."
—John 21:15-17

Food is nourishment and entertainment; it's also sharing and an expression of values and the nurturing of life. When Jesus tells Peter to feed his sheep, he's telling us to feed one another. We are reminded that we are both shepherd and flock.

I'm told that shepherding is a hard, boring job. I know that the unrelenting task of meal planning, shopping and cooking can be tedious and difficult. But if we allow the routine to calm us, then we can breath in God's love and embrace the world around us as we wait at the grocery checkout line, chop vegetables for dinner or bake a special holiday cake. Feeding the hungry— even the hungry we love most—will change us if we respond to God's grace.

HEALTHY APPLESAUCE CAKE

1½ cups unsweetened
     applesauce
1½ cups rolled oats
1¾ cups raisins
1 cup butter
1½ cups raw sugar
2 eggs, beaten
2 cups unbleached flour
½ cup soy flour (or substitute
     unbleached flour)
2 tsp. baking soda
2 tsp. cinnamon
½ tsp. ground cloves
½ cup walnuts or pecans,
     chopped (optional)

ICING
2 cup powdered sugar
16 oz. cream cheese
1 tsp. vanilla

In a saucepan heat the applesauce, rolled oats and raisins. Stir frequently while heating. Bring to a boil, then remove from the heat and cool to room temperature. Meanwhile, cream together the butter, sugar and eggs in a bowl. In a separate bowl, sift together the flour, baking soda, cinnamon and cloves. Mix the applesauce and butter mixtures into the dry ingredients in small portions and mix after each addition. Add ½ cup chopped walnuts or pecans if desired.

Pour the batter into two greased and floured 8- or 9-inch round cake pans (or in a large sheet pan if you want to carve the cake into a Christmas tree, an angel or an Easter lamb). Bake at 350° for 25 to 30 minutes. The cake will crack a little on the top and an inserted toothpick will come out clean when it is done.

To make the icing, soften the cream cheese to room temperature. Mix with powdered sugar and vanilla. *Serves 12.*

The question of bread for myself is a material question, but the question of bread for my neighbor is a spiritual question.

NIKOLAI BERDYAEV

EATING WITH SINNERS

And as he sat at dinner in Levi's house, many tax collectors and sinners were also sitting with Jesus and his disciples—for there were many who followed him. When the scribes and the Pharisees saw that he was eating with sinners and tax collectors, they said to his disciples, "Why does he eat with tax collectors and sinners?" When Jesus heard this, he said to them, "Those who are well have no need of a physician, but those who are sick; I have come to call not the righteous but sinners."—Mark 2:15-17

Jesus calls us to engage in the world. When he ate with tax collectors and sinners, he didn't pretend they weren't sinners. He challenged their motives and invited them to change. Those couldn't have been comfortable meals.

The guests at these meals represented the institutions of the day. In our own lives, our guests represent our institutions—even though they may not be major players. It's by talking together that we and our guests will change and, when we leave the dinner table, take on the task of living our lives differently.

A just society begins with us. As we change our hearts and minds, we can begin to influence a change in others by discussing our concerns with friends and colleagues and by organizing our efforts within our communities through economic boycotts, protests and voting blocs. Work to persuade others to do the right thing. That is what Jesus did, and he tells us to follow him.

Making chocolate chip cookies with off-brand chocolate morsels always reminds me of the power of boycotts. Bake them often for inspiration!

CHOCOLATE CHIP COOKIES

2¼ cups all-purpose flour
1 tsp. baking soda
1 tsp. salt
1 cup butter or margarine,
    softened
¾ cup sugar
¾ cup brown sugar, firmly
    packed
1 tsp. vanilla extract
2 eggs, beaten
1 12-oz. pkg. semisweet
    chocolate chips
1 cup nuts, chopped

In a small bowl combine the flour, baking soda and salt. Set aside. In another large bowl combine the butter, sugar, eggs and vanilla. Beat until creamy. Gradually add the flour mixture. Stir in the chocolate chips and nuts. Drop level tablespoonsful of the dough onto greased cookie sheets. Bake at 375° for 8 to 10 minutes, or until cookies are brown at the edges. *Makes 5 dozen cookies.*

How may times, all through my life, have I surveyed these tables full of people and wondered if the bread would go around; how many times have I noticed how one heaps his plate and the last one served has little, how one wastes his food and deprives his brother.

DOROTHY DAY, from *Loaves and Fishes*

THE LORD IS SWEET

And they gave him a piece of broiled fish, and of an honeycomb.—Luke 24:42
(King James Version)

In Luke's account of Jesus' last appearance to the apostles and disciples, Jesus shows them his wounds, asks for food, imparts a little more knowledge and then leads them to Bethany, where he is taken up to heaven. The passage above is from the King James Version of the Bible. In the New Revised Standard Version, the disciples simply give Jesus a piece of fish. That is perhaps a more accurate account, but the prayerful commentator or scribe who added the honeycomb in the King James translation expresses our need to give something sweet back to God.

No feast is sweeter than Christmas. The scene of the infant in a manger, surrounded by his parents, stable animals, shepherds, choirs of angels and the three kings sweetens our hearts. We remember our own innocent participation in Christmas skits and drape our children in sheets and shawls, smiling as they pretend that the family dog and cat are a donkey and a sheep.

These tender moments form a honeycomb of textured, sweet experiences. We call our loved ones, "honey," "sugar" and "sweetie pie." And the thick honey and chewy comb call up an image of simple pleasures and the genuinely sweet moments in our lives. The moments we have remind me of another King James translation: "Taste and see that the Lord is sweet" (Psalm 34:8).

CHOCOLATE CHOCOLATE SWEETS

CRUST

1¾ cups flour
⅓ cup cocoa
¼ cup sugar
1 tsp. salt
1½ sticks butter (¾ cup), chilled
⅓ to ½ cup strong coffee, chilled

FILLING

12 oz. semisweet chocolate chips
⅔ cup sugar
2 tsp. Kahlúa (coffee liqueur)
2 tbs. milk
2 tbs. butter, melted
2 eggs
½ cup chopped walnuts
48 walnut halves (optional)

Crust: sift together the flour, cocoa, sugar and salt. Add the chilled butter, cut into small pieces. Using a mixer or a food processor, mix until the ingredients resemble coarse crumbs. Gradually add the chilled coffee. Knead briefly; wrap and refrigerate several hours or overnight. Then cut the dough into quarters, and roll each on a well-floured board to a thickness of about ⅛ inch; keep remaining dough chilled. Using a 3-inch-diameter cutter, cut circles in the dough and press them into the cups of lightly greased, tiny muffin tins (measuring 1¾ inches across each cup). Refrigerate while you prepare the filling.

Filling: place the chocolate chips in an oven-proof bowl and place in the oven at 200° until the chocolate melts. Remove from the oven and increase oven temperature to 350°. Stir the sugar, Kahlúa, milk and melted butter into the melted chocolate. Beat in the eggs until the mixture is smooth. Stir in the chopped walnuts.

Place 1 tsp. of the chocolate mixture into each crust-filled muffin cup. Bake for 20 to 25 minutes, or until tops are firm. After removing the pans from the oven, top each sweet with a walnut half, and allow them to cool in the pan for 15 minutes. Remove from the pans to finish cooling on racks. *Makes about 4 dozen.*

BE READY FOR ACTION

*"Be dressed for action and have your lamps lit; be like those who are waiting
for their master to return from the wedding banquet, so that they may open the
door for him as soon as he comes and knocks. Blessed are those slaves whom
the master finds alert when he comes; truly I tell you, he will fasten
his belt; and have them sit down to eat, and he will come and serve them."*
—Luke 12:35-37

Our yearly Christmas vigil reminds us that we are living in the age of
the Second Coming. Christ is born every minute of every hour, not
just on the 25th of December. At Christmas Eve vespers we pray, "The
Lord shall come. Run to meet him, the Almighty, the All Powerful, the Prince
of Peace. For it is the great beginning, and of his kingdom there shall be no
end." Luke tells us that our attitude should be watchful and prepared. We
must be ready for action whenever the Lord appears. And if we are, he will, in
turn, serve us. How much more willing, then, we should be to serve one
another.

As delivery carriers, peddlers, baby-sitters, beggars, relatives and friends
arrive at our door during the holidays, be prepared to meet them with a smile
and serve them a warm welcome. It's Christmas. It's always Christmas. This
lemon poppy seed cake is good any time, but it's especially enjoyable when
shared with company.

LEMON POPPY SEED POUND CAKE

light vegetable cooking spray
1 tsp. flour
½ cup margarine, softened
¼ cup sugar
¾ cup water
¾ cup egg substitute
¼ cup frozen lemonade
    concentrate, thawed
1 tbs. lemon rind, grated
2½ cups flour
2 tbs. poppy seeds
1 tsp. baking soda
1 tsp. baking powder

LEMON SYRUP
⅓ cup powdered sugar,
    sifted
4½ tsp. lemon juice

Coat the bottom and sides of a 9-by-5-by-3-inch loaf pan with cooking spray. Dust with 1 tsp. flour.

In a large bowl, cream the margarine while adding the sugar gradually. Beat until creamy. In a separate bowl, combine the water, egg substitute, lemonade concentrate and lemon rind. Stir well. Sift the flour, baking soda and baking powder into the creamed margarine a little at a time, alternating with some of the lemon mixture and mixing each addition thoroughly. Then add the poppy seeds. Pour the batter into the pan and bake at 350° for 50 minutes or until a toothpick inserted into the center of the cake comes out clean. Remove the cake from the oven and prick the top at 2-inch intervals with a fork.

Cook the lemon juice and powdered sugar over medium heat until the sugar dissolves, stirring constantly. Pour the lemon syrup over the cake. Cool in the pan for 10 minutes, remove and cool on a wire rack.

Do not neglect to show hospitality to strangers, for by doing that some have entertained angels without knowing it.
HEBREWS 13:2

THE COOK'S SIMPLE PRAYER

And the Word became flesh and lived among us, and we have seen his glory, the glory as of a father's only son, full of grace and truth.—John 1:14

God became human and lived among us, literally "pitched his tent among us." Being human meant God had to eat, drink and sleep. He had meals prepared for him and prepared meals for others. Indeed, he became a sacrificial meal for all of us. He used images of food and agriculture to teach us about repentance, justice, mercy, serving others, the nature of the spiritual life and the kingdom of God. Cooking remains a chore for most of us much of the time, but we can infuse it with meaning if we so choose.

Our work in the kitchen is a labor of love. It's a good place to grow in our consciousness of God because it offers us the possibilities of mystical contemplation. Whether our meals are the simplest of foods or demanding works of art, the act of cooking can lift our hearts and minds in simple prayer. Jesus calls laborers, saying, "Come to me, all you that are weary and are carrying heavy burdens, and I will give you rest. Take my yoke upon you, and learn from me; for I am gentle and humble in heart, and you will find rest for your souls. For my yoke is easy, and my burden light" (Matt. 11:28-30). This promise of rest and relief applies to our work in the kitchen as much as anyplace else. Take Jesus at his word.

FRUIT CRUMBLE

4 lb. mix of soft fruits (such as apricots, peaches and kiwi) or hard fruits (such as apples and frozen berries)
2 tsp. cornstarch
2 tbs. lemon juice
²/₃ cup white flour
¾ cup brown sugar
¹/₈ tsp. salt
1 tsp. cinnamon
¼ tsp. nutmeg
5 tbs. butter
2 tbs. ice water
1 cup rolled oats

Wash and pit the fruit. Peel if desired. Slice and layer in a glass baking dish, 13-by-9-inch. Mix the cornstarch and lemon juice and pour over the fruit.

Combine the flour, sugar, salt and spices. Cut the butter into the mixture with knife until the mixture resembles coarse cornmeal (or use a food processor). Sprinkle in the ice water and mix with a fork. Add the oats and mix again until it is well combined and forming little clumps. Sprinkle the topping evenly over the fruit.

Bake at 475° for 30 minutes or until the top is crisp and brown and the fruit juice is bubbling.

We go to the kitchen to be nourished and revealed. It is a holy place.

GUINILLA NORRIS, from *Becoming Bread*

Acknowledgments

I'm grateful to Steve Dierkes for his meticulous and intellectually demanding reading of my work; he sharpened big ideas, tightened sentences and corrected many errors. I'm also grateful to Rev. Jim Krings, a student of scripture, who reviewed my exegesis and encouraged me to be "experimental and imaginative in your spiritual life as well as in your cooking." Several cooks shared recipes with me. Kathy Sullivan, S.L., tested many, helped me search out the best and maintained unflagging interest in this project. Jeff Wunrow, another fine cook, read all the recipes for clarity. After all this help, if any errors or muddy thinking remain, they are my own.

Index to Recipes

anchovies, with pasta, 133
aspic, tuna, 91
Argentinian Stew, 131
avocado, and shrimp, with pasta 19
Baked Salmon with Tomato-Basil Sauce, 73
Baked Ziti, 119
balsamic vinegar, with sautéed spinach, 93
Basic Creole Fish Stew, 17
beans
  black bean soup, 21
  Italian bean salad, 79
  refried, 25
Bean Sprouts, 81
Berries with Creamy Yogurt Cheese, 103
Black Bean Soup, 21
Blue Cheese, Mushroom and Caramelized Onion Pizza, 15
borscht, raspberry, 77
bread
  challah, 63
  Irish Soda, 47
  Italian Soda, 47
  multigrain, 43
  Russian soda, 47
  starter, 35
  white, plain, 37
bread machine, 41
buns, hot cross, 59
burritos, spinach, 25
cake
  applesauce, 145
  fruit, 143
  pound, lemon poppy seed, 151
carrots, ginger, 109
casserole, spaghetti, 29
catfish, fried, 71

Challah Bread, 63
cheese
  blue, pizza, 15
  brie and roasted garlic, 85
  cheddar, with honey bran muffins, 53
  creamy yogurt, and berries, 103
  feta, with watermelons and olives, 95
chicken, stir-fried, 135
Chitterlings and Hog Maws, 121
Chili Rellenos, 67
chili, vegetarian, 31
Chocolate Chip Cookies, 147
Chocolate Chocolate Sweets, 149
cider vinaigrette, with sweet potatoes, 129
Cloverleaf Rolls, 38
cookies, chocolate chip, 147
Corn Tortillas, 49
crab, imitation, spinach salad, 75
  with quiche, 125
Cranberry Soup, 121
crumble, fruit, 153
crust
  pie, 141
  pizza, 45
Egg Foo Yung, 81
eggs, hard-boiled, 61
  quiche with crab, 125
Eggplant Salad, 89
Eggplant Swiss, 23
eggplant, stuffed, 113
Fast Buttermilk Yeast Rolls, 55
fish
  catfish, fried, 71
  crab, imitation, salad, 75

crab with quiche, 125
shrimp and avocado with pasta, 19
salmon, baked, with tomato-basil sauce, 73
scallops, with lettuce salad, 97
shrimp with wild rice, 101
stew, creole, 17
tuna aspic, 91
Fresh Tomatoes and Roasted Garlic Pasta, 99
Fried Catfish, 71
fruitcake, traditional, 143
Fruit Crumble, 153
garlic
  roasted, and brie, 85
  roasted, pasta, 99
Ginger Carrots, 109
ginger, pureed, preserved, 109
Granola, 107
grape leaves, stuffed, 137
gumbo, turkey, 121
Hard-boiled Eggs, 61
Healthy Applesauce Cake, 145
hog maws, and chitterlings, 120
Honey Bran Muffins with Cheddar Cheese, 53
Hot Cross Buns, 59
How to Make a Starter, 34
Imitation Crab Spinach Salad, 75
Irish Soda Bread, 47
Italian Bean Salad, 79
Italian Soda Bread, 47
lamb
  leg of, 57
  stuffed in grape leaves, 137
lasagna, vegetarian, 117

Leg of Lamb, 57
Lemon Poppy Seed Pound
     Cake, 151
lemon sauce, 113
lettuce salad, with scallops,
     97
Mango Salsa and Chips, 87
Melitzanosalata (Eggplant
     Salad), 89
muffins, honey bran, with
     cheddar cheese, 53
Muffins with Oatmeal,
     Walnuts and Dates, 51
Multigrain Bread, 43
mushroom, pizza, 15
Norwegian Julekaka, 47
olives, and watermelon, with
     feta cheese, 95
onion, caramelized, pizza, 15
pancakes, potato, 27
Pasta Primavera, 69
Pasta with Anchovies, 133
Pasta with Shrimp and
     Avocado, 19
pasta
     lasagna, vegetarian, 117
     garlic, with fresh tomatoes,
        99
     sauce, 115
     spaghetti casserole, 29
     ziti, baked, 119
pepper sauce, roasted, 113
pie, pumpkin, very low fat,
     141
pizza, with blue cheese,
     mushroom and onion,
     15
Pizza Crust, 45
Plain White Bread, 37
pork, roasted in milk, 127
Potato Pancakes, 27
potatoes, sweet with cider
     vinaigrette, 129

Pureed, Preserved Ginger,
     109
Quiche with Crab, 125
Quick Pasta Sauce, 115
Raspberry Borscht, 77
Rice with Stir-fried Chicken,
     135
rice
     white, 135
     wild, with shrimp, 101
Roast Pork in Milk, 127
Roasted Garlic and Brie, 85
rolls
     cloverleaf, 38
     fast buttermilk yeast, 55
Russian Soda Bread, 47
salad
     eggplant, 89
     imitation crab spinach, 75
     Italian bean, 79
     lettuce, with scallops, 97
salmon, baked, with
        tomato-basil sauce, 73
salsa, mango, 87
sauce
     lemon, 113
     quick pasta, 115
     orange-ginger, 111
     primavera, 69
     tomato, 115
     tomato-basil, 73
     roasted pepper, 113
Sautéed Spinach with
        Balsamic Syrup, 93
Scallops with Lettuce Salad,
     97
shrimp, and avocado with
        pasta, 19
Shrimp with Wild Rice, 101
soup
     black bean, 21
     cranberry, 121
     turkey gumbo, 121

Spaghetti Casserole, 29
spinach, salad, imitation crab,
     75
     sautéed, with balsamic
        vinegar, 93
Spinach Burritos, 25
sprouts, bean, 81
squash, stuffed, with orange-
        ginger sauce, 111
starter, bread, 35
stew
     Argentinian, 131
     basic creole fish, 17
Stir-fried Chicken, 135
Stuffed Squash with Orange-
        Ginger Sauce, 111
Stuffed Eggplant with
        Roasted Pepper Sauce,
        113
Stuffed Grape Leaves, 137
Sweet Potatoes with Cider
        Vinaigrette, 129
tomato sauce, 115
Tomato Seasoning Mix, 115
tomatoes, fresh, and roasted
        garlic pasta, 99
tortillas, corn 49
Traditional Fruitcake, 143
Tuna Aspic, 91
Turkey Gumbo, 121
Using a Bread Machine, 41
vegetables, springtime, with
        pasta, 69
Vegetarian Chili, 31
Vegetarian Lasagna, 117
Very Low Fat Pumpkin Pie,
     141
Watermelon with Olives and
        Feta Cheese, 95
ziti, baked, 119

Index to Scripture Passages

Hebrew Scripture
Gen. 2:9, p. 65
Gen. 41:34, p. 30
Gen. 41:35-36, p. 116
Lev. 3:16, p. 118
Lev. 20:24, p. 66
Num. 11:5-9, p. 44
Deut. 10:17-19, p. 120
Psalm 34:8, p. 48, 148
Psalm 104:14-15, p. 42
Prov. 28:3, p. 68
Prov. 30:8, p. 21
Eccl. 3:1-5, p. 87
Eccl. 9:7, p. 101
Song of Sol. 5:1, p. 102

Christian Scripture
Matt. 2:11, p. 140
Matt. 3:4, p. 18
Matt. 3:11-12, p. 123
Matt. 4:3-4, p. 50
Matt. 4:18, p. 70
Matt. 6:11, p. 40
Matt. 6:16-18, p. 36
Matt. 7:16, p. 105
Matt. 9:9-13, p. 84
Matt. 9:35-38, p. 106
Matt. 11:18-19, p. 88
Matt. 11:28-30, p. 152
Matt. 13:3-9, p. 112
Matt. 13:24-30, p. 110
Matt. 13:33, p. 33
Matt. 16:5-12, p. 13
Matt. 17:24-27, p. 74
Matt. 22:1-14, p. 92
Matt. 23:23, p. 134
Matt. 25:37-40, p. 126
Matt. 26:17-19, p. 56
Matt. 26:26, p. 48
Matt. 27:50-51, p. 58

Mark 1:30-31, p. 26
Mark 2:15-17, p. 146
Mark 4:26-29, p. 114
Mark 7:26-30, p. 90
Mark 9:49-50, p. 14

Luke 1:53, p. 139
Luke 5:33-35, p. 86
Luke 5:37-38, p. 100
Luke 8:51-55, p. 20
Luke 9:12-17, p. 24
Luke 10:5-11, p. 94

Luke 10:38-42, p. 130
Luke 11:11-13, p. 16
Luke 11:37-41, p. 98
Luke 12:16-21, p. 142
Luke 12:24, pp. 11, 22
Luke 12:35-37, p. 150
Luke 14:1, 14, 15, 24, p. 83
Luke 15:23-24, 29-31, p 96
Luke 19:1-10, p. 136
Luke 24:30-35, p. 62
Luke 24:42, p. 148
Luke 25:55-56, p. 60

John 1:14, p. 152
John 2:1-11, p. 128
John 4:7-8; 28-29, p. 132
John 4:13-14, p. 132
John 4:32, p. 132
John 4:35-38, p. 108
John 6:5-14, p. 46
John 6:8-9, p. 72
John 6:25-27, p. 38
John 6:48-51, p. 34
John 6:68, p. 74
John 12:1-8, p. 130
John 21:9-13, p. 124
John 21:15-17, p. 144

Acts 2:42-43 p. 54
Acts 2:44-47, p. 28
Acts 14:15-17, p. 80
I Cor. 3:1-3, p. 76
I Cor. 10:16-17, p. 52
II Cor. 9:6-8, p. 78
Eph. 3:16-19, p. 129
Heb. 13:2, p. 151

Additional Resources from ACTA Publications

Cooking from the Heart. On three separate video tapes, host Barbara Valentine teams up with top chefs to demonstrate how to cook healthy, tasty dishes. These broadcast-quality videos add a spiritual dimension to standard TV cooking shows. Sprinkled throughout each video are scripture verses about food, nourishment and meals that lead viewers to reflect on how God fills their lives with everlasting spiritual food. A printed list of ingredients for the recipes is included with each video. Order all three volumes together and save 10%. Comes with automatic 10-day preview.

> **Volume I, Bountiful Sea** (60 minutes, eight seafood recipes, $19.95)
> **Volume II, Bountiful Land** (60 minutes, eight meat and pasta recipes, $19.95)
> **Volume III, Bountiful Feast** (30 minutes, four main dish recipes, $14.95)

Daily Meditations (with Scripture) for Busy Moms by PATRICIA ROBERTSON. A wonderful, down-to-earth, daily meditation on the spirituality of motherhood is illuminated by a carefully chosen verse from the Bible. Companion volumes available for busy **Dads**, **Grandmas**, **Grandpas**, and **Couples**. This bestselling series is sure to delight anyone interested in the spirituality in family life and relationships. (368 pages, $8.95 each)

Home Is a Holy Place: Reflections, Prayers and Meditations Inspired by the Ordinary by MARK G. BOYER. More than thirty reflections on ordinary household items such as aprons, keys, water, zippers, tables, pillows, mailboxes and electricity. Each meditation is accompanied by a relevant Bible passage and an original prayer to help bring people to the realization that their home is indeed a sacred space, that Christ is always the unseen guest at their table, and that the divine presence is truly at home in their home. (88 pages, $6.95)

Precious Jewel Person: Reflections on the Spirituality of Everyday Life by BARBARA RITTER GARRISON. A book about the holiness of everyday life: the chance encounters with God, the challenge of relationships, the humor and the sadness of the human condition. To all this, the author brings the sensibilities of the artist and the wit of the stand-up comic. (133 pages, $8.95)

Available from booksellers or call 800-397-2282 in the U.S. or Canada.